'I've known Mick for a long time, and I've seen at first hand how lives are being transformed through his profoundly pastoral ministry at Church on the Street.'
William Ash, actor

'Pastor Mick is a gift from above, and the journey he continues to make lifts my soul. He walks among strangers to become friends with everyone he meets ... May his story inspire others to give back what God has given us all.'
Chris Difford, musician and songwriter

'Fleming is a living testimony to how human beings can break the cycle of destruction and transform their lives to bestow good upon others. Through these true, often extraordinary stories, Mick reminds us of the forgotten, and opens our eyes to real-life suffering that many are unaware of.'
Hannah Gal, journalist and award-winning documentary film-maker

'Mick's incredible story stopped me in my tracks the first time I heard it. Now he writes from the heart to share his experiences in a way that gives hope and inspires us to take action.'
Dr Andrew Ollerton, theologian, pastor and popular communicator

'For years I've watched Mick's journey unfold, at times full of hope inspired by his church, and at his lowest in despair at the human suffering he has witnessed. I've seen the impact of his ministry on him personally, visiting him in hospital when he was close to death in spring 2023. But what has never changed is his resilience to carry on, with the unwavering belief that there is more good than bad in the world, and it is the good that will triumph.'
Ed Thomas, UK Editor, *BBC News*

***

Praise for *Blown Away*:

'There are so few people like Pastor Mick that this book deserves a shelf all to itself.'
Jeremy Vine, broadcaster and journalist

'Mick Fleming's story is at the same time both unbelievable and real. It reveals a man who was dreadfully wronged and guilty of many wrongs – yet miraculously found forgiveness and the ability to forgive. Liberated from bitterness and guilt, Mick's response has been to do more good in one lifetime than a whole roomful of politicians. A gritty, gripping and moving book.'
Tim Farron, MP, leader of the Liberal Democrats, 2015–17

From the Foreword to *Blown Away*:
'It's impossible to visit Church on the Street and not be deeply moved by the work the organisation does for those in need.'
HRH The Prince of Wales

Bishop Mick Fleming has a degree in theology from the University of Manchester and was ordained into The International Christian Church Network (TICCN) in March 2019. He is Bishop of TICCN and of Church on the Street in Burnley, a Christian community dedicated to helping others, particularly those who find themselves homeless, struggle with addictions or are on the bread line.

Bishop Mick's autobiography, *Blown Away* (SPCK, 2022) was a bestseller. It has been published in French (*Rédemption: Du deal à la vraie Vie*, MAME, 2023) and German (*Schonungslose Gnade: Meine Geschichte von Täuschung, Erlösung und der Kraft der Vergebung*, SCM Hänssler, 2024), with a Dutch edition forthcoming in spring 2025.

PASTOR MICK FLEMING

WALK IN MY SHOES

STORIES OF MIRACULOUS TRANSFORMATION

First published in Great Britain in 2025

SPCK
SPCK Group
Studio 101
The Record Hall
16–16A Baldwin's Gardens
London EC1N 7RJ
www.spckpublishing.co.uk

British Library Cataloguing-in-Publication Data
A catalogue record for this book is available from the British Library

ISBN 978-0-281-08792-1
eBook ISBN 978-0-281-08793-8

1 3 5 7 9 10 8 6 4 2

Typeset by Fakenham Prepress Solutions, Fakenham, Norfolk NR21 8NL
First printed in Great Britain by Clays Ltd

eBook by Fakenham Prepress Solutions, Fakenham, Norfolk NR21 8NL

Produced on paper from sustainable sources

For the children and families of those who have struggled with addiction

Contents

List of plates

Credits

Photograph 19: © Pool / Getty Images
All other photographs: The family's collection

1
'YOU'LL NEVER WALK ALONE'

I SLAMMED ON THE BRAKES. My passenger jolted forward; then, like a dead weight, he hit the back of his seat. With the engine still running I jumped out the car, leaving the door just hanging there in the breeze. A mad dash to the ripped shoes that were poking out from the shrubbery, exposed by the sunlight. *Here I am*, they screamed.

And there he was. In a distorted sleep, bedraggled but still breathing, alongside yellow flowers that almost matched his complexion. A dark brown bottle by his side acted as a prism, sending a shimmering haze of light across torn jeans. So much beauty amid so much despair.

The traffic thundered past, but if you attended closely, you could begin to make out the troubled journey those battered shoes had been on. And their final steps before they stopped and just lay down to die.

I knelt by his side and whispered gently, 'Do you want to live?'

He opened his eyes. Piercing blue. Not what I expected. I had to turn away just for a second to catch my breath.

'You're Michael,' he said.

In the silence that followed, my mind began to ask how he knew my name but nothing came out of my mouth.

'You're Archangel Michael.'

Ah! Well, I am Michael but I'm no angel, that's for sure.

'Listen, take your shoes off. I need to swap,' I said.

Something happened in that exchange. Water began running from his eyes in a gentle release. And as peace wrapped itself around us, I noticed the tall shadow that had been towering over us had shrunk. I turned to see my passenger sobbing, with his head in his hands.

Back in the car it was like a spark had been ignited. A fire was burning in my friend.

'I've never seen anything like that before,' he said.

'It's just a pair of shoes, but I know who they really belong to.'

My friend was so very touched that his journey changed, his path was reset. He walked away in new shoes too.

That made three of us.

* * *

Almost a year later my old shoes found their way home. I spoke to an empty chapel as it welcomed another sinner who had finally met his angel. The yellow flowers illuminating the coffin danced in my heart as the dark velvet curtains began to close.

For me, death has always been near. Only ever a touch away. By the time I was twenty, four of my closest friends had died, and my lovely kind sister was gone. Death became something I simply waited for. I craved darkness so much, I could hear my footsteps getting louder as I neared the gates of hell. Faces would come at me out of the darkness, unable to speak, yet calling me with groans of fear, anger, bitterness and hatred. But then, just as I willingly began to take a step forward, the gates were slammed shut.

I found myself in a place full of light – right there in my car! The bottle in my hand, tinged with blood, completely lost its allure, and I fell on the floor, tears streaming from my blind eyes, washing away the darkness … I remember the sky looking as I'd never seen it before. Somehow bluer, a radiant azure ocean, with clouds moving peacefully across, almost like an armada of ships just disappearing from view.

From that moment, death seemed to lose all power over me.

I was dying to live, not living to die.

It seems that death can shine a light on life itself.

* * *

I'm fifteen. Hanging out with a friend the same age. We're planning how to make vast fortunes and what we'll buy with our imagined wealth. He lives rough and I just want to be anyone but me. He passes over a smoke, hand-rolled and sprinkled with the antidote to pain. As I breathe in, my brain changes channels and a temporary peace caresses my mind. Everything slows right down, almost as if we've stopped time itself … Just for a moment, I'm pain free and the fact that we're sitting in his home – an old, dark air-raid shelter just off the bottom of the back street – doesn't seem to matter.

Many moons later, he walked into Church on the Street, and we flung our arms around each other, reigniting the flame of companionship once more. He stayed in my life for the next two years. Alcohol had become his master and when it called, he would always answer, right up until he took his last drink.

No money means no funeral, no goodbyes – unless I could just dig deep. I prayed and God answered. The undertaker dressed him in one of my old suits and a pair of brown shoes donated by my friend Gordon.

A funeral, but not for the faint-hearted. You see, if you're having a service where all the mourners are alcoholics, 3:30 in the afternoon is a bad idea … Trying to carry the coffin into the church without permission and almost dropping it; two mourners ending up on the floor, with bottles clunking and the hiss of ring-pulls; people walking up and down the aisle like we were in the pub. And all the time, the noise just getting louder and louder.

The undertaker cowered at the back as arguments erupted over who owed who what and how much. The stern-faced crematorium manager whispered in my ear in a panic, 'What shall we do?'

I didn't respond. I simply gazed at twenty or so grieving men and women who didn't know how to feel.

Then, at the top of my voice, I shouted, 'Quiet! Have some respect!'

The atmosphere calmed right down. Heads bowed as I left the pulpit and encouraged every person to come to the front. As we joined hands, the music played 'You'll Never Walk Alone' and our out-of-time and out-of-tune voices almost blew the roof off! The Holy Spirit fell and rivers of tears ran from tired eyes as our hearts responded. The undertaker was in shock. The manager cautiously peered around the door as the certainty of 'death being defeated' was celebrated and became so infectious that joy was birthed. As I said a final prayer, you could have heard a pin drop.

I realised in that moment that every step we take in life can be a step nearer to home or a step further away.

It all depends on whose shoes you're wearing.

2
THE RED SHOES

MY EARLIEST MEMORY is of something that was etched into my brain, and the passing years have coloured it in, making it brighter, more vivid and alive. I still wonder how a seemingly trivial incident could have created so powerful an image in such a young child.

I was six years old and quite a mummy's boy – mummy's little soldier, marching round the house like a fearless general.

'Get ready, we're going out, Michael.'

It's so funny how I can still hear that voice, even after all this time.

'OK, Mum.'

On with the glasses, the ones with the frosted lens. You see, I was a good boy, me. I had progressed from the sticky plaster with the yellow line down it, almost glued over one eye. I glanced in the mirror and thought how strange I looked, a feeling that's never really left me. I ran downstairs, ready for inspection.

'Come here, love, you've got a tidemark round your neck.'

I wondered how I could have a tidemark when I'd never even been to the seaside, but Mum knew best. She spit on a flowery handkerchief and violently rubbed my neck and face as I wiggled like one of the worms in the backyard.

'That's it, all done!'

A wonderful adventure on a bus to Manchester. As we got on, the driver smiled at me and I smiled back. When I shouted, 'Mum, that man's got a black face,' his smile turned to a laugh, but Mum squeezed my hand a little tighter, just to the point where the pain was enough to shut my mouth. I never really understood why.

We jumped off the bus and I dragged her to the kiosk – all the coloured sweets were looking at me through their glass jars and I could choose anything I wanted. Sherbet lemons, the ones with the ridges on, the ones that fizzed on your tongue.

Mum let go of my hand to delve into her magic bag and fish for that brown leather purse. I turned round, just for a second and … there she was! The most beautiful sight my frosted glasses had ever seen. I'm sure if they hadn't had those silver hoops holding them behind my ears, they would have jumped right off my face.

She must be a real princess. Her red shoes with high heels were so shiny and bright. They made my heart beat just a little faster. My eyes began to climb her legs, one black square at a time. She reminded me of the red fire engine in my toy box, with the black ladders on the back. Her hair was golden and full of curls. Her lips matched the shoes and they smiled at me. In that moment, I think I would have given her all my sherbet lemons – well, most of them anyway.

Her eyes were the blue of those ice pops you could get from the corner shop and looked as if there were spiders round them. *She must live in a castle or a palace*, I thought. She was even more beautiful than my sister's dolls.

Maybe she's an angel.

When she bent down, I could see her knees. I'd never really noticed knees before.

'Hello, what's your name?'

'I'm Michael. Are you a princess?'

She smiled and nodded.

I knew it! I knew she was.

Just at that moment, Mum turned round and grabbed my hand. The familiar squeeze that I didn't understand, and that sharp jolt as she dragged me away.

I looked over my shoulder. One of the spiders waved at me. I tried to wave back but my eyes seemed not to work one at a time. As we left, I could still smell that sweet smell – a princess smell, even better than the smell of sherbet lemons.

'You don't talk to ladies like that, Michael, do you understand?'

'But she's a princess, Mum.'

'No, she's not.'

But I knew she was because she told me.

All the way home I kept thinking about the princess, her hooped earrings that swung backwards and forwards as she moved her head, and the gold cross that hung in mid-air as she bent down to talk to me. It had Jesus on it.

I wondered why Mum didn't seem to want to look like a princess too, but I didn't ask – I'd had enough hand squeezes for one day.

* * *

Many years later, I found out that not all princesses live in palaces.

Sherbet lemons had become white rocks and I had become

11

a twenty-five-year-old drug addict, searching for something, somehow, somewhere.

It was on one of these missions that I met another princess.

'Looking for business?'

'Get in!'

She smelled of perfume – you know, like too much of it? Her tights were torn at the knee but the shoes looked the same – bright red high heels – though scraped and scratched. Her gaunt white face and deep-set eyes told me she was exactly what I was looking for.

'Listen, love, I've got plenty of cash. All I want is to score some crack and go somewhere to smoke it. Nothing else. Are you up for it?'

I knew she was, even before she spoke. That twitch of the head, that tight jawline, told me she just needed to melt.

'Can I get some gear to come down on afterwards?'

'Yeah, course you can.'

I put my hand in my pocket to feel the wrap of notes there. It felt safe just flicking my thumb over the ridges of the paper. Money seemed to have a power over my emotions that people simply didn't.

She must have been about twenty. Her voice was calm, almost a whisper, but you somehow felt it had the potential to unleash hell. She had pale skin, which made the bruises on her arms and shoulders stand out all the more. Each could no doubt tell a story sad enough to bring a tear to most souls – but not to this one. I was more concerned about getting my hands on the beautiful glistening white stones that would take me to my heaven.

As we spoke, I looked down at her fingernails. Expertly painted, pale purple, flawless – almost like a work of art.

As she tapped on the hem of her short denim skirt, I was reminded of the heather that blows in the breeze on the hill in my mind; a place of peace that I've never really been to, yet craved all my life. When the tapping stopped, I could see the scorch marks on the ends of her fingers, the consequence of burning rocks and running brown lines across silver sheets of foil.

I had a strange feeling later when she took hold of my hand. She was gentle. It was almost like when you're little and your mum holds your hand, but different somehow. A complete stranger gently leading me into a dark dismal flat. I felt for the cold steel in my pocket, just in case. A deep breath as she relocked the front door and my eyes viewed safety. I let go of the steel and just relaxed. I spent two days with her there. We shared stories, fears, hopes and of course drugs together.

As we were coming down, she said, 'Will you hold me in your arms?'

'Well, I suppose so.'

Her bones were sharp and hard. She smelled of sweat and perfume. The essence of heroin lingered still, and a lamp with its shade askew made a cock-eyed shaft of light on the wall. She rested her head on my chest and, as I put my arm around her shoulder, the lamp seemed to glow brighter as a sweet sound filled the air. She was singing to me. I didn't want her ever to stop. She was like an angel.

Peace flooded into my soul as I *felt* something! Her voice cut through years of anger and the pain that had somehow lodged itself in the pit of my stomach. At that moment she changed. She became a princess. I think I might have cried, but I wasn't able to back then. I felt her tears run down my chest and then, so softly, I heard her pray for me. I didn't know what to do or say. This tiny princess had slayed the dragon in me. I was beaten; lost in her heavenly voice. In that moment, if I'd been able to choose to spend the rest of eternity feeling this way, I'd have taken it. I slipped into a beautiful, relaxed serenity as the sound of 'Amazing Grace' filled the room and my soul.

Time passes, and memories can become a distant echo of a different you that feels gone for ever. Yet, sometimes a face, a call or a song reopens the door. As it did for me.

* * *

It was almost the King's coronation. Sarah and I had been invited to Buckingham Palace. Sarah got a new hat! I got a new suit! We sat in the palace gardens in the sunshine, watching all the beautiful ladies getting their high heels stuck in the lush lawn. That made me smile. We glimpsed the King and Queen and a real princess. You see, some princesses do live in palaces after all.

The brass band belted out tunes without words, the music somehow complementing the perfectly cut sandwiches laid out like diamonds in a jeweller's shop. The tea tasted different, not like it does at home – its special blend spreading warmth through my whole body.

I looked over the top of my china teacup at Sarah. She was so beautiful. She was smiling, not at anything in particular, but just because she was happy.

The beefeaters in their red uniforms formed a guard as the King and Queen walked slowly across the garden to greet some of the guests. I looked back at the palace over a sea of multi-coloured hats, and breathed in a million different perfumes. I saw a rainbow reflected through a crystal glass of juice, and it occurred to me that it doesn't matter who you are or where you are, the sun will shine wherever it likes.

Yet, how many two-up two-downs would fit into Buckingham Palace? How many homeless people could be housed in its spare rooms? I began to feel troubled and uneasy in this world of the royals. And then I remembered welcoming the royals into my world: the Duke and Duchess of Cambridge, just as we were coming out of the pandemic, sitting round the table at Church on the Street, discussing the work that we do, and how it could be replicated across the country. That brought a smile to my face. The Prince of Wales (as he now is) has basically nicked some of my best ideas! But it's all right – many people are going to benefit. And, after all, he is the future king.

But for now, something my brain just couldn't process: Lionel Ritchie to my left and the King and Queen of England to my right! I tried so hard to say hello to Lionel; the temptation was so great. As I slurped my cuppa, the words formed in my head: *Hello, is it tea you're looking for?*

Fortunately, I decided to leave them right there. Such a special experience for me and Sarah. As we left the palace, she held my hand and gently kissed me on the cheek. I know I've found my real princess, one who could live anywhere, from a park bench to a palace, and that makes me feel like a prince.

As we travelled home, I carefully arranged all the photos I'd taken and then hit social media, creating memories and blue ticks to tell me I was doing OK. I'm still a bit needy, you see. King and Queen, superstar singers, and me and Sarah.

Ding!

A message.

My heart contracted. A moment of confusion, even though I recognised the name.

'I've been following you for a few years, but seeing the pictures of the palace just now ... I guess we've both come a long way.'

I clicked the needy button to check the account was real. Hundreds of thousands of followers! But she had sung for me; she had cried on my shoulder all those years ago. Suddenly I was back in that hellhole, hearing the sweet, sweet sound of 'Amazing Grace' that almost broke my heart.

Looks like the prayer has finally worked. The bruises have healed up. The smell of heroin has disappeared. The chains have been broken. We've both been set free.

These days I can cry, my heart is soft.

These days we both wear different shoes.

An international award-winning singer and a bishop.

Touched by God's amazing grace.

3
THE ACCIDENTAL PREACHER

THEY HELD EACH OTHER in the darkness, wrapped in dirty sheets, praying that tonight they would be invisible and the familiar, distorted shadow would somehow pass them by. The bedroom door was slightly open, allowing a slice of light to hit the wood chip on the wall. It looked like rice pudding but smelled of fear, just like the stains on the mattress.

The sound of creaking floorboards on the landing. Thoughts too dark for a five-year-old girl and a four-year-old boy to understand.

'Close your eyes, Thomas, think of Jesus.'

Her tiny warm fingers grasped his as they began to pray in a whisper.

'It's working,' she said.

The wood chip disappeared and silence returned to the room. Clara sat up, her brown eyes so used to the darkness, nail-bitten hands clutching a picture of Jesus holding a lamb.

'Are we like that lamb?' Thomas asked.

'Yes, Jesus is looking after us, Thomas.'

Thomas and Clara would scurry around the house, searching every inch to find pictures or medals of Jesus to protect them. Thomas had a little statue of Jesus that showed his heart, and when the shadow came to wrap itself around him, Thomas would squeeze the statue tightly and say, 'We love you, Jesus, we love you, Jesus', over and over again.

They would stay awake all night talking to Jesus. They knew that the longer they prayed, the shorter the abuse would be next time – and they were always right. When the next time came, they would imagine Jesus taking them by the hand and leading them to a special place, where they could run and play in the tall grass, wild flowers dancing in the breeze, laughing, warm and safe.

Evil entered their bedroom for many years, holding them but never owning them. Touching their bodies but unable to touch their innocent souls. Lost children who had forgotten how to play but learned how to pray.

'Clara, does this happen to all kids?' Thomas asked.

'I think so,' she replied, 'but we're very special, Thomas, because we've got Jesus.'

By the time Clara was seven, she had become almost a mother to Thomas, her childhood stolen and buried in a shallow grave.

* * *

Through her school years, Clara's need to feel safe and protected became an obsession. Her mind lied to her, saying everything would be OK if the house was in order; if things were scrubbed with bleach, she'd be made clean again. Such holy rituals consumed her. The false god of OCD took residence in her mind, working in her every waking moment, even distorting her dreams. It would not listen to reason, and finally, she had no bargaining power left. She was lost.

As time passed, Clara became a real mother, but even the need to love and protect her children couldn't still her troubled mind. The taste of alcohol seemed to push her fears away, but not for long. Feelings of impending doom would always return. There were short respites as she sank deeper into drug and alcoholic stupors, days and nights passing without significance, memories being deleted, hopes and ambitions lost. Her only consolation was the children.

But Clara had tried to be a mum from the age of seven, and now she was all mothered out. In reality, her need for love was just as great as her family's. They were all searching for something they just couldn't find. Eventually, the children were removed and Clara, feeling life had nothing left to offer, simply craved death.

Yet, somewhere deep inside, there was a light … so dim and far away she could hardly make it out.

* * *

A new obsession overtook her. She had to get the kids bikes for Christmas. It would be a final act, showing how much she cared for them before they went into full-time foster care. Her mind swirled and pondered … She couldn't steal the bikes. She had no money to buy them. But she felt she had to find a way, even though there was nothing left, nothing to sell, nothing to give.

Clara was alone. Thomas was in prison – again. The legacy of his childhood trauma was a propensity to petty crime, and he'd become a prolific offender. But at least he was safe.

A sudden fleeting memory of her little brother asking, 'Are we the lamb, Clara?' prompted her to cry out. For a moment, she was a child again too.

'Jesus!'

Then a waterfall of pain and tears.

'If I am the lamb, save me from the wolves, Lord. Help me, forgive me.'

* * *

Upstairs on a double-decker bus that evening, Clara rested her tired head against the window. The glass felt nice and cool, and the mild judder of the engine seemed to soothe the aches in the rest of her body. Droplets of rain sparkled in the streetlights' glow, and two teenage girls in the back seat laughed as they practised the hand movements of a dance. Clara glanced round and saw there were dreams of stardom on their faces. But their smiles were real. She almost smiled herself, remembering another young girl's dreams from long ago.

Outside, a man in a cream raincoat held his collar up as his face got pelted with rain. A lady in a red coat seemed to fare better, flicking her hair back and gliding along the wet, puddly pavement. Then the bus stopped: wind whistled up the stairs as footsteps and a thud preceded the appearance of a face, swiftly followed by the whirl of a can of beer rolling across the floor. A man's trembling hand retrieved it, much to everyone's relief. Clara nodded. She knew that feeling only too well. Pain always recognises itself.

Nervously twisting and rolling her ticket between her fingers, Clara rang the bell to get off. Suddenly, she was desperate for a cigarette. The bus shelter gave little protection as she struggled to get it alight, but when the tobacco had finally taken hold, she noticed a neon light reflected in one of the panels. A new boldness overtook her. Swerving the traffic to cross the road, she smoothed back her hair, took a deep breath and pushed open a heavy black door.

Warmth, glitz, shimmering lights!

A plush reception area with a pretty girl behind the desk helped Clara feel safe. Confidently she asked, 'Do you need any girls?'

'I think we do. Is this your first time looking for this type of work?'

Clara's head was bowed almost in prayer as she answered in a not-so-confident whisper, 'Yes.'

'Sit down and I'll get the boss to look at you.'

Clara felt her stomach contract. But the boss seemed to be favourably impressed.

'Stand up,' he said. 'Turn round. Oh yes, you look a bit Spanish. You'll do. Start tomorrow night, eight o'clock.'

That was it. The kids would get their bikes. Sometimes there's nothing left to sell but the self. Emotions melt away and reason blinds itself to truth. A dangerous place for anyone to live.

* * *

Despite her daily battles, Clara's protective instinct remained strong, and she continued to visit Thomas, who was often still in prison, whenever she could.

During a period of release, he met two street preachers from America. They prayed over him, but he ended up stealing one of their mobile phones. As a result, Thomas was sent back to prison for two years, but on an IPP (Imprisonment for Public Protection) sentence. Such sentences were more usually intended to safeguard society against dangerous offenders, who could be held for up to ninety-nine years.

IPP sentences were abolished in 2012, but sadly for Thomas, those handed out before that were not lifted. He has never committed an act of violence, and his mental health has been affected so badly, he's developed schizophrenia. Thomas should be in hospital receiving treatment but remains in prison, thirteen years after his last offence.

IPP prisoners have, in fact, been classed as torture victims, and Clara has become an activist, joining with other families in the fight for justice. Her passion has taken her to the House of Lords, the House of Commons and the High Court of Justice. At times, she has felt alive again, yet the fight has left many scars.

Once, when she was at an all-time low and didn't know which way to turn, Clara sought me out at Church on the Street. She told me she felt the IPP campaign had become an obsession, and that she'd turned away from God. As I listened to her, I assured her that was not the case. God fights against injustice and he wants to set the prisoners free.

'You've become the accidental preacher.'

Clara was transformed by these five words. She realised she *was* doing God's work. She asked me if I could help her, because no church leaders at that time would get involved – they all said the issue was too political.

To be honest, that was music to my ears!

The first thing we did was get Clara on to The Exodus Project, an abstinence-based drug and alcohol programme I'd written. She developed a different perspective, and it was a joy to see her begin to go about her work (as the great Salvation Army hymn has it) 'in the strength of the Lord'.

Our next task was to devise a strategy for Clara to have an audience with Lord Blunkett. He was the Home Secretary when IPP sentencing was brought in; understandably, Clara resented him deeply. At their meeting, however, Lord

Blunkett was profoundly apologetic and said he'd do everything he could to help. Thomas had never been allowed by the prison system and social services to see his son. So, true to his word, Lord Blunkett intervened, and now Thomas and his teenager son have regular prison visits.

Clara is grateful for small mercies. But the battle to have Thomas moved into psychiatric care, where he can get the real help he needs, continues.

Sadly, there are still over fifteen hundred others with similar stories. Almost a hundred people have taken their lives while on IPP sentences, and the number grows year on year.

Lord Brown was a justice of the Supreme Court between 2009 and 2012, and this is what he wrote in a foreword to a report on the impact on those recalled under the IPP regime:

> I have no hesitation in describing the continuing aftermath of the ill-starred IPP sentencing regime as the greatest single stain on our criminal justice system ... Whether detained under their original sentences or recalled [IPP prisoners], together with their families, exist in a Kafkaesque world of uncertainty, despair and hopelessness, indefinitely detained unless and until they are able to satisfy the inevitably difficult test of persuading the Parole Board that they can safely be (re) released. Our reputation as a just nation demands that this IPP stain be at last eradicated.[1]

True justice must always have space for mercy, otherwise justice becomes injustice. We continue to pray for Thomas, knowing that in God's eyes, he is the lamb held in Christ's loving arms.

* * *

Postscript: The publishers had already passed this chapter on to the copy-editor when Clara rang me one morning.

'Did you put in the bit about Jonesy?'

'You know, love, I don't think I did.'

It's a little story well worth hearing, so here it is.

Clara sent a copy of *Blown Away* to Thomas in prison, and he loved it. He's always been a Christian, but as I've explained, he's had a troubled life, and hearing how God has worked so miraculously in mine was a real comfort.

In fact, Thomas was on segregation (kept apart from all the other prisoners) when he received the book. The guy in the next cell, Jonesy, was driving him crazy, screaming and shouting all day and all night.

When they were out on exercise one morning, Thomas offered to lend him *Blown Away* to help pass the time.

But Jonesy just laughed. 'I'm not like you lot. I don't believe in God. I'm an atheist.' Then he started talking some really dark stuff.

The next day, sick of the banging and the insane shouting, Thomas tried again. And miraculously Jonesy replied, 'Oh, go on then.'

For two days straight, no one heard a peep out of him.

It didn't last.

'Here we go again!' Thomas groaned.

But Jonesy was shouting for the chaplain. And when the chaplain came, he asked for rosary beads. He wanted to give his life to Jesus.

Thomas was gobsmacked. He's been in prison for so many years and he's never seen anything like this.

Jonesy got out of segregation before Thomas. He's never returned the copy of *Blown Away*, and Thomas is really miffed about that.

He thinks God probably wants Jonesy to have it anyway!

4
THREE IN ONE

'DO YOU WANT SOME BREAKFAST?'

I shook my head, and the metal hatch slammed shut with a clang that pierced my eardrums. My mouth was like sandpaper. Maybe I should have asked for a brew after all.

The wooden bench I'd been sleeping on was hard; the only covering a single sheet so rough it had grazed my cheek. As I rose unsteadily to stretch my arms and legs, reality kicked in. A cold police cell on a Saturday morning. A pervasive sense of nothingness mingling with the stink of stale alcohol and tobacco. My body shaking on the inside.

I'd give anything for a can of cider right now!

I began to count the blue painted bricks on the walls around me. It became an obsession. I had to get to a thousand. I just couldn't stop. Nothing else mattered.

Then a key hit the lock and the heavy metal door swung open.

'Come on, son. Interview time.'

I couldn't move, I was only at eight hundred bricks.

A pause. 'Did you hear me? Move it.'

Nine hundred – close now.

'Out, or I'll drag you out.'

One thousand. *Phew, that's better.*

Last night's drugs had made things a bit blurry. I was eighteen and about to become a father. I'd had my first detox at seventeen, but no one had ever told me I was an alcoholic. Strange, really, that I'd never worked it out. I was certainly the architect of my own demise.

Welcome to manhood, Michael, the voice in my head said. *Let's count some more bricks …*

* * *

My thoughts were interrupted by the band playing 'Amazing Grace'. Almost forty years later, there I was, microphone in hand, standing at the front of the church about to take the service. So many faces, old and young, were looking back at me that the temptation to count the chairs was strong. The fact that the rows weren't in straight lines was jarring my brain. Then the sound of those sweet words declaring that my chains had gone, I'd been set free, and my God and Saviour had ransomed me,[2] and I was drawn back to sanity – or at least what passes for sanity with me.

My eyes scanned the room. On my left Ajani (not his real name), my son's friend from Kenya; on my right Nadia, a young girl whose father had converted from Islam, sitting with him and her mum. No cells or drugs for them. Just teenagers praising God.

I wished for a moment that I could have had their lives at eighteen. Then a feeling of shame and sorrow swept over me. Their stories weren't all sunlight and roses; they were about pain and endurance. Nonetheless, their journeys were in Christ. Mine had been in a bottle, running from … what? I didn't really know.

My eyes met Ajani's and the light in them penetrated my soul. I looked proudly at my son Daniel alongside. His compassion and need for justice had birthed a friendship that was based on the love of God, not on the need for stuff or reassurance.

'Dad, I've met this lad from Kenya. Do you think the church might be able to help him?'

'Well, son, we'll try.'

Daniel had taken me to meet the young refugee at the place he was living, an immigration house. His room was clean and neat and I noticed two pictures on the wall, one of Jesus and one of the Blessed Virgin Mary. They were coloured in with crayons. I could see that Ajani had very little in the way of possessions, but the Spirit of God ran through him, exuding a type of gratitude and humility I've rarely perceived in one so young.

Daniel is a good amateur runner (probably my obsessive genes, put to better use!), and one day, he found Ajani walking around the track where he trains. Through the wonderful Google Translate, it transpired that Ajani wanted to compete with the other runners but had no money to join the club. Daniel brought him to his coach, who said, 'Let's see if the kid can run.'

Oh my! With no diet, no training, no adequate trainers or clothes, Ajani smashed all the club records without breaking a sweat.

'He's got real potential to be a top athlete, Dad.'

'What does he need?' I asked.

It was decided we would take Ajani to church and hook him up with the lady who works for us assisting refugees. We began teaching him English and lent our support to his application for immigration status in the UK. After searching around, Daniel found a small amount of sponsorship, enough to buy his friend running shoes and shorts, and to help with his diet.

Within a few months, Ajani was running the fastest time for under-twenty-year-olds in the UK, and meeting some of the faces who were the future of athletics. These were people with massive sponsorship deals with Nike, Adidas and all other leading sports brands. Unfortunately for Ajani, he can't travel until he's been granted immigration status, so he relies on kindness and the love of God to support his efforts. This year, the U20 world athletics championship was in Lima. Ajani obviously couldn't go to Peru to compete, but when we saw the gold medal winning time and compared it to his last race, the realisation that he was multiple seconds faster than the gold medallist just about blew our minds!

'Could Ajani win a gold medal for Great Britain one day, Danny?'

'It's more than possible, Dad, yes.'

The government moved Ajani to a new house, and guess what? It's right next to a professional running track. Sometimes you just can't make these things up.

I wondered how Ajani had ended up in the UK. Daniel told me that, due to some kind of political problem, his dad had been murdered. With no one to support him in his running, the families of his wealthier running friends knew the boy was doomed if he stayed in Kenya, so they clubbed together to get him a flight to the UK. He was found on the streets here, just trying to survive. Now Daniel's seeking to give Ajani the opportunity to realise his potential.

When I was eighteen, I guess I was on a journey to nowhere; Ajani, on the other hand, has a very clear goal in mind. I spent more than two-thirds of my life trying to run into the past; Ajani is running into the future. Maybe one day he'll walk into Church on the Street holding an Olympic gold medal. Maybe he'll just live out his life in the love and peace of Christ. Either way, he's a winner.

As the apostle Paul said: 'Do you not know that those who run in a race all run, but one receives the prize? Run in such a way that you may obtain it' (1 Corinthians 9:24). All we've ever dreamed of will be ours if we run for Christ, keeping our eyes on him. Yet, I never stop wondering how people manage to go on in the midst of trauma …

As we hit the last chorus of 'Amazing Grace', I could see Nadia with her hands in the air, praising the Lord. Her dark eyes were aglow, but part of her face was in shadow; alive in Christ, yet living in the most debilitating physical pain. This is a little of her story.

Hi, my name is Nadia and I'm seventeen years old. I was raised a Muslim, but my dad became a Christian when I was ten, and my brother and I were baptised. Four years earlier, I was diagnosed with juvenile arthritis, which meant I couldn't do sports or play fast games or go on school trips and things like that. It's been hard for others to understand that I can't walk without pain or stiffness.

In a way, I'm sometimes almost happy that I have this limitation, because it keeps me humble. It reminds me that, though the flesh is weak, the spirit can never be defeated by disease. It helps me see what matters. When I'm ill, there's more room for God. All the same, sometimes I get angry and upset, and when Mum gets a phone call from the hospital about my latest tests, I feel anxious in case they say something bad.

Before my dad became a Christian, he took amphetamines, and there was a lot of anger in our home. I still feel traumatised that my parents didn't behave in a loving way to each other when I was younger. Though I tried to keep it in, I spent a lot of time crying in my room, and I used to tell myself I couldn't wait to leave home when I was eighteen. Now, though, my dad is a changed man, completely off drugs, and I love having my parents around. They're like my best friends.

At Church on the Street, we preach a gospel of powerlessness, and this young girl has had a huge impact on us all. Nadia can't change her circumstances. She's been close to death with sepsis, and she understands her own mortality because of that. Naturally, she's scared of dying.

And yet, it's like the daily pain she's in is a gift to the rest of the world. In a strange way, she allows you to see God through her suffering. Almost without realising it, she ministers to her own parents. It's been glorious to witness Adam and Katherine being changed by their interaction with their own daughter, and they've become a crucial part of our ministry at Church on the Street.

* * *

Mick, Ajani and Nadia. Three stories. Three very different journeys.

Each in the loving company of one relentlessly devoted God.

5
'I SHOT THE SHERIFF'

'YOU BETTER SIT DOWN, Dad, I've got something to tell you. You won't like it.'

My heart sank. I looked Jack straight in the eyes and waited for the body-blow.

'I don't know how to put this ...'

'Just spit it out, son.'

The next few moments seemed to take for ever. My mind darted to various scenarios: he's got a girl pregnant ... or maybe he's going to tell me he's gay. How will I react? What should I say?

'Well, Dad, you see, after Mum died I really wanted to go to university. I've applied and got in.'

'What do you mean I won't like it! That's brilliant. Well done, son! Which university?'

'Derby.'

'Fantastic – your mum would be so proud of you.' I felt the muscles in my cheeks relax as a smile of relief wiped itself over my face. 'So, what are you studying? Don't tell me. Bet it's sports science, isn't it?'

Jack looked apprehensive. His eyes refused to meet mine and he was biting his bottom lip. 'Not quite, Dad.'

A pause.

'It's policing!'

'For a moment there, I thought you said policing.'

'Yes, Dad, I did.'

The silence was just long enough to be uncomfortable.

Well, no one is pregnant, and he's not gay. But a copper! My son wants to be a cop. Coppers have been the enemy all my life.

'Why do you not like the police, Dad?'

Jack really challenged me with his question. Why have I had this prejudice all my life? What's really at the root of it?

Late that night, in conversation with Ozzy the wonder dog, we worked out that it all stemmed from my rebellion against authority.

Ozzy's a great listener. Doesn't say much, but that stare speaks volumes.

* * *

The next morning, outside in the sun with a coffee, I was watching life go by when the silence was broken by two little boys playing with plastic guns. I wondered who was the goodie and who was the baddie. (I hoped when they grew up they wouldn't swap their toys for the real thing; boys need to learn new games when they become men.)

In an instant, my mind had transported me back to the early 1970s ... As a small child, I was obsessed with cowboys and Indians. How real and serious our games were! I smiled as I recalled a victory.

The backstreet had been transformed into the wild west. The sheriff was wearing a brown cowboy hat, and the sun shone so brightly you could see the gold star on his chest reflected in Mrs Dent's shiny green gate. He had two metal six-guns in his holsters; I had a plastic knife and tomahawk.

That sheriff's going to get it, I thought.

I straightened my headdress and one of the feathers tickled my face. But I was ready! A brave chief with his weapons drawn. My yells were terrifying as I put my hand over my mouth, on and off, on and off, and ran straight at the bewildered sheriff. I looked him in the eye and he froze for a second before reaching for his shiny silver pistols.

Too late.

In one mighty swoop, I dived on him with all my might. He fell to the ground and dropped one of his guns. I grabbed it and blasted him; the caps exploded and the smell of gunpowder filled the air.

'I shot the sheriff!' I shouted.

The sheriff began to cry. He ran home to tell his mum. I looked down and saw his brown cowboy hat lying on the concrete and in one last act of defiance, I jumped on it. It felt good. Then I legged it all the way to our back gate and on into the kitchen.

'Where've you got that gun from?' my mum asked.

'I found it.'

'Well, it's not yours. Go and put it where it was.'

Just at that moment, the sheriff's mum knocked on the door. I could see her through the bubbly glass.

'Jean, your Michael's took my lad's gun. Please can he have it back.'

Mum grabbed the gun and handed it over. 'So sorry, I'll speak to his dad.'

That was me in trouble again, but I didn't care. I shot the sheriff! I was a brave warrior, even though I didn't get any supper that night.

As it turned out, I'd face many sheriffs down the years and, like me, they didn't always fight fair.

* * *

My first arrest was at the age of nine.

Reflecting now, I'm shocked at how young I was to be committing a criminal offence. I broke into a dark blue Austin Maxi outside the bus depot, round the corner from our house. It was teatime, and the light from the orange street lamp revealed a big cardboard box on the back seat of the car. It's strange to say, but there's always been a part of me that feels that seeing something I want makes it mine by right. I'm not stealing; I'm taking what already belongs to me.

My excitement grew as I tried the heavy door handle. Oh, the joy when it opened! I climbed in and managed to drag my prize out on to the pavement. As I pulled back the flaps of the magic box, it was like opening a very special present. My excited hands rooted around and I pulled out … a pair of black high heels, tied together with string, something like my big sister would wear. Then pair after pair … My first proper heist: a box full of ladies' shoes.

The obsession subsided as the disappointment hit. Then I noticed a small brown bottle with a white cap on the front seat. I reached over and grabbed it and gave it a shake. The sound made me feel good, so I shook the bottle a few more times. I tried to open it, but I just couldn't get through the lid. I dropped it on the pavement and jumped on it with my trendy black wedges. A cracking sound and I was in!

Beautiful white tablets shimmered like stars under the street light. I picked one up and wondered what would happen if I swallowed it. Maybe I would become big and strong, like a superhero. The temptation was too much. I popped the tablet into my mouth and waited a moment for something to happen, then reached for another just to be sure …

And take off!

But not how I expected. I was lifted bodily as a deep voice boomed, 'Oi!!' One of the bus drivers dragged me to the depot and locked me in an empty office. I felt scared. I knew my mum was going to kill me. I was really in trouble now. What on earth was I going to do?

Jailbreak!

It took me just ten minutes to climb up on a table and lift a chair on top. When I managed to open the window, I could taste freedom … They didn't even know my name, after all. I leapt from the sill, and as my wedges hit the tarmac, I did a little roll. They do that in the movies, you see.

Unfortunately, at that very moment a panda car pulled up. A hand grabbed the back of my jacket.

'What's your name, lad?'

'I'm not talking till I've seen my brief.' I didn't know what it meant, but that was what you were supposed to say, I thought.

'We'll see about that, son.'

Once I was down at the station, I had an overwhelming sense of doom. I might never see my mum and dad again. I was sure I was going to have to live on bread and water for ever. No more chips or Mum's jam slice. I felt so sad that I began to cry.

'Will I get the electric chair?' I said to the policeman, the one with no hat on.

'No, son, not this time.' He was holding back a smile.

When Dad came to get me, I felt even more scared. I didn't know if he was angry, or just pretending to be. Grown-ups are like that, you see; you just can't tell. I hadn't done anything wrong. I was only playing. The police were picking on me, I thought.

'What's he arrested for?' the custody sergeant asked.

'Armed robbery.'

They wouldn't get me next time!

But they did.

I can see now that in many ways I was the perfect victim. Those who have read *Blown Away* will understand that what happened two years later – and its tragic consequences – possibly had a horrible inevitability about it. Misplaced trust and a natural waywardness are a very dangerous combination in a child.

* * *

Jack is my youngest. In a sense, his upbringing was far tougher than mine – he has nine half-brothers and -sisters – and yet growing up, his mum Lyn doted on him, attending to his every need. The devastating impact of her cancer diagnosis when he was sixteen was compounded by the fact that he was quite lacking in household or practical skills. He had no idea how to cook and couldn't even identify the lawn mower in the garden shed, let alone cut the grass with it.

And yet, over the next two years, Jack rose to the challenge. He nursed his mum while holding down a job in a super-market to try to make ends meet. He trained as a cage fighter, and found the discipline helped him emotionally and gave him a focus. He learned to cook and to take care of himself. Yet, as his mum grew frailer and frailer, I felt we had to have a conversation. I needed to reassure him – and maybe myself …

'Jack, you know your mum's going to die. No matter what happens, you'll always be able to stay with me. You'll always have everything you need.'

He cried when she passed away at home, her body ravaged by the disease. Most of Jack's childhood friends by that stage were skilful criminals, but Jack's intrinsic strength of character meant he had matured enough at eighteen to take a different path.

On 17 July 2024, I posted a picture of him on X with the caption: 'This young man is Jack. His father was a drug addict; he nursed his mother as a boy while she died of cancer. Today he graduated with a [BA Honours] degree [in policing]. I'm so proud of you, son.'

That post has touched over 150,000 people. Jack's story shows what young people can achieve, despite the odds.

As for my childhood adversary … well, he went on to become a policeman and did me for several minor offences.

But I'm OK with that. Because it was me who shot the sheriff.

6
THE BISHOP'S SHOES

I SAT AT HOME in my favourite chair, the one that's moulded to fit me perfectly, my best friend at my side with his head on my shoulder. Ozzy the wonder dog. The fountain of knowledge. The one who always runs to me, the one who never lets me down.

We looked outside at the birds battling through the wind and listened to the gentle rhythm of the rain dancing on the window. Ozzy lifted his head to follow a coke can as it shook and rolled, as though to tease him.

If I could stop time and be in this moment for ever, I'd take it. The truth is that's not possible, but even if it were, I wondered, would that be freedom for me?

I didn't know, but maybe Ozzy did.

Perfection was broken in a moment. Ozzy bounced off the chair and shook the room as my phone lit up like a Christmas tree.

No caller ID.

'Hiya, Mick, how's things?'

'Good. Thanks.'

A second-long mind delay before I realised who it was. My old friend calling from prison. He's served nine years already and has another three to go before he's even eligible for parole. I wondered what freedom looked like for him. He's different now. I don't think prison rehabilitates people, but it

49

does change them. Is there a good way of learning that the old is gone and accepting the truth of the present? How does that relate to our dependency on one another, and could it be that mutual dependency is a source of real freedom?

* * *

When I was told I was going to be consecrated as a bishop, three things came to mind that I had never heard a bishop say:

1 'I wonder what it would be like to smoke crack after all these years.'
2 'Blimey, she's got lovely legs.'
3 'He really could do with a smack in the mouth.'

All humans have contradictions within them. The love in me doesn't want me to hide the darkness. The light of Jesus sets me free to speak out, to rejoice in the freedom of sin dying in me, and I don't ever want to pretend – pretending can't be living. I do have fleeting thoughts of death and cutting myself to release pressure. But these days, that's all they are. Fleeting thoughts with no power. I don't live in them. Christ has freed me.

The joy of knowing this consumes me sometimes. When we articulate our struggles and difficulties, we give other people permission to confess and repent and be healed. I pray for the day all bishops can say, 'He could do with a smack in the face.'

That's real freedom, because vibrant faith is to be found everywhere – even in a prison cell.

Wearing bishop's shoes has wrought a strange transformation. I've always thought that, no matter what, I'd better be where God's putting me. And if that involves being 'bishopified', then that's what I ought to do, even though I don't look 'bishopy'.

Indeed, on the day of the consecration I confess to wondering, *What on earth am I doing wearing a strange pointy hat and my grandma's curtains around my shoulders?* And as I stood there, fully robed, in front of the bishops, a representative of Her Majesty the Queen who was getting ready to speak, my dear friend Ed Thomas from the BBC who would read his tribute, and Will Ash from the TV soap *Emmerdale* who caught my eye, I thought, *How extraordinary ...*

Then from the back of the church came the immortal words: 'Get your ******* hands off me.'

And there she was. A little pack of dynamite with no fear, her dark hair stuck to her pale face, her body cold, her hands blue. Literally. You see, when you're homeless and wet, life drains from you. Justice seems invisible and all hope seems to die. What she was shouting was so poignant and filled me with so much love, I felt my feet fit perfectly in my new shoes.

'Why is he getting made a bishop when I'm sleeping on the streets?'

With an understanding of the context and the perspective, this was an amazing question. At the perfect moment.

'Why does he wear hundreds of pounds' worth of robes while I go hungry? Why are you all here and no one's helping me?'

Worried faces flashed glances across the church. Rescuers rushed forward, trying to calm her. Bishops looked on in horror, but no one could answer her questions. Not one. I'm sure God sent her just for me. I felt I knew the answer. I was so at peace in that moment. It was like time had stood still.

I wrapped my arms around her and felt her cold body begin to relax as tears fell. She held me tight, and the tears turned into sobs of hope as she whispered in my ear, 'I'm so cold, Mick. I'm so hungry I don't know what to do.'

That was the moment I knew I was the right kind of bishop for what God had called *me* to do. Love melted and warmed her, clothed her, fed her and eventually found her a house, a place of her own where she could just be herself. A place where she felt safe. A place where, a few weeks later, she fell asleep and didn't wake up. A place where God called her home.

Before she died, she heard a song about Calvary and came to ask me what Calvary was. She found out it was a place of transformation, a place of hope, a place of love. She sang that song so well. Her passing and her funeral touched many, many people, and a bishop laid her to rest.

She found her own Calvary and I found a new peace.

A new peace given by a woman who followed the cries of pain deep down inside herself and came and shouted them out in front of God.

Maybe that's real freedom.

7
PRIVILEGE AT A PRICE

I'VE SEEN PROSTITUTES serve the Lord in the most remarkable ways. I've watched addicts give their last pennies to help another addict. I've witnessed the hungry feeding the hungry, the abused comfort the broken, and heard murderers preach the gospel with life-transforming power.

I've been rich and I've been poor, but now everything I have just seems to pass through my hands to where it's most effective.

In my ministry, I've met many wealthy and famous people, and one thing that's really struck me is that privilege comes at a price. Thinking about it, I've never met a rich person who strives to be poor. I have met many poor people who strive to be rich, and it seems to me that money definitely plays a part in the decisions we make and the choices we opt for in life. Indeed, the haves and the have-nots have many things in common. Among the most important, I believe, are an ability to pray, an ability to give, and an ability to receive. Surely a good life would balance all three.

Why is there a tendency for us to feel that rich people have perfect lives? Many criminals I've known over the years have taken risks to gain wealth. Some have managed to keep their freedom; others have been sent to prison or died because of the consequences of their actions. All were in pursuit of more, I'm sure, than just money. I've known famous people who have achieved wealth, but it's transpired that their passion has actually been for something else, such as sport, art, music or drama. Some time ago, when I spoke to Prince William, I found he seemed to be driven by duty – to our country and its people. It's intriguing that everyone I've encountered has been influenced to some extent by their past – sometimes a positive past, sometimes a negative past, but usually a mixture of both.

I believe the gospel of Jesus Christ doesn't make the rich poor; it makes the poor rich and the rich humble. It's remarkable really, this gospel message. There's no cash required! What a leveller.

* * *

I received a request to speak at a prestigious private school. Feeling these young men and women really wouldn't relate to my story, I was about to decline, when Sarah said, 'Do it – you might learn something!'

I smiled. I'd been caught out again. She's good like that, Sarah. She sees right through me and gently pushes me back in line. So humbling to know that you can go anywhere and learn something; so arrogant to think that you're always the one there to give rather than receive. Maybe that's the power of the gospel.

As I pulled up at the gates of the school, the sheer splendour of the place struck me. The grounds were bigger than any council estate I'd ever seen, and the buildings were off the scale. *There you go again*, I thought, noticing my old prejudice returning. I was quite pleased I'd caught myself this time, with no help from Sarah!

I walked down oak-panelled corridors, past works of art, and through a beautiful hand-carved doorway into a room with chairs laid out in perfect rows – I noted with satisfaction! – twenty in each. The teacher greeted me and shook my hand. Her perfume reminded me of my mum (I could just picture the Chanel No. 5 bottle … Dad would buy it for her in the duty free when they went on holiday, and it would last at least a year). The teacher seemed a nice lady, in an outfit that was smart but not quite what you might expect in such grand surroundings. Her flat black shoes, proper teacher's shoes, stepped up onto the dais, and she introduced me.

The hall was full of boys and girls between sixteen and eighteen years of age, whom I deemed to be 'privileged'. Many would likely go on to be captains of industry, lawmakers and governors of the future. Just for a moment, my eyes lifted towards the ornate plaster mouldings on the ceiling, and I thought, *What the hell am I doing here?*

A deep breath and I began to speak. There was no mic, but the natural acoustics in that ancient place (Oliver Cromwell had walked the corridors before me!) were remarkable. The idea was that I would share something of my testimony and then go on to talk about the work of Church on the Street. Five minutes in, I was conscious of what sounded like sobbing, followed by some quiet mumblings. Paradoxically, the silence seemed to get louder. You could have heard a pin drop as these immaculately dressed young men and women nodded in agreement with my story. This wasn't what I had expected at all.

When I finished speaking, I said, 'If you'd like to ask any questions, please fire away.'

No one uttered a word. Everyone seemed shell shocked.

The teacher spoke gently. 'If what Pastor Mick has said has affected you at all, please talk to one of the pastoral staff.'

It seemed that a private word with me was more what these young people desired. I was overwhelmed by the number who gathered to see me afterwards, each of them hovering patiently until others had had their turn.

I remember one girl saying, 'Pastor Mick, I know exactly how you felt when you were young, because I felt the same: all alone.'

I was humbled, and a little bit ashamed of myself, but I managed to ask what she meant.

Her eyes welled up. 'I've been sent to boarding schools all over the world since I was eight years old. I've been separated from my family. I felt so alone growing up.'

Another boy confided, 'This is the first time I've realised that great wealth and great poverty can exist so closely together. A fifteen-minute drive away, the world looks so different.'

All afternoon (and in many subsequent emails), I heard similar stories of self-realisation, and saw worldviews being shattered right before my eyes. If these young people were privileged, then they were paying the piper quite a price for it. I guess if you have money, you can be miserable in comfort, or bring comfort to the miserable. Yet measuring yourself by what you have, or even by what you've achieved, will never bring fulfilment. There's too much internal conflict, because we're called to use what we've been given, not to be used by it. Whether people are rich or poor, in good health or bad, the love of God, rather than the love of stuff or of self, is the truth that will set us free. It sounds easy. Until we forget. And forget. Over and over again.

* * *

Sarah was right. I did learn something I hadn't expected. The phrase from Alcoholics Anonymous's Big Book sprang to mind: 'contempt prior to investigation'. I need to be very careful about coming to conclusions before I've all the facts.

Another school day for me. Still learning!

8
GRANDAD'S CLOGS

'WOULD YOU LIKE ANY SAUCES?'

'No thanks, love, I'm fine.'

The clatter of cutlery punctuated the murmured conversations, the tap tap tap of laptops, the occasional rustle of a newspaper ... a comforting soundscape that seemed to match the swirling sea of beige in my teacup. Then a fleeting memory: Dad in his dark blue work clothes, a cigarette in one hand, his white pint pot of builder's tea, with black bits at the bottom, in the other. I touched the top of my head as I recalled his calloused hand roughing my hair, his smile ... Putting his cigarette out in the shiny blue Embassy Regal ashtray. Pretending to throw a punch. Me ducking and holding my hands in a fighting position. I think six was a good age to practise being a man.

I felt a wave of nostalgia sweep over me. A deep sense of loss as I realised just how much I miss him.

Dad is still a part of who I am. But these days my rations are poached eggs on brown toast, no sauce, and a modest cup of tea. How things change! No pint pots any more. No bacon, egg, sausage, black pudding and fried slice, swilled down with coffee the colour of tar ... I suppose nothing stays the same. Life moves and twists and turns, and takes us with it.

It looked dismal outside, but the café was bright and warm and I could see the faces of two young boys reflected in the window. Beside them sat their dad, oblivious to his surroundings, hypnotised by the social media ticks on his phone. He speared a piece of bacon and almost missed his mouth.

'Dad, would you rather be invisible or be able to fly?'

No reply.

The boys instinctively answered their own question as their father periodically looked up to take a slurp of coffee. One shouted out excitedly, 'I'd rather fly!', while the other held a chip like an aeroplane and landed it perfectly in his mouth.

As I drove home, I wondered how my dad would have responded if I'd asked him the same question. I think he would have said, 'Don't be bloody stupid. You can't fly and you're not bloody invisible.'

Harsh words, but you see, he knew me. He knew my potential to jump off a roof flapping my arms; to try to steal his wallet as I practised being undetectable.

Then I wondered about my grandad. How would he have replied if Dad had asked the same question when he was six? As I turned the steering wheel to pull up outside my house, I felt my nose judder and a tear sploshed on my arm.

My grandad wouldn't have been there to ask. He was a very troubled man. I felt so sorry for my dad, and so sorry for my grandad. And then I had a revelation.

I was just like my grandad. I had been an alcoholic who wasn't present for his family. It was not a nice feeling at all. I felt a twisting and turning, a bonding and connecting, a recognition of experiences shared. A shadow from far, far back appeared to stretch across time. It was almost as if my DNA was unravelling …

I began to understand that I am not just part of my own past.

I am part of my ancestry.

* * *

William Fleming was a proud Irishman from County Mayo. He worked the land and he loved horses. In my mind, he probably nicked one or two as well! Irish rebel songs were a happy part of my childhood … My dad with curly black hair and me sat on his knee as he sang, his voice tinged with the raspy sound of whisky. Giving me a little sip to drink and laughing at the way my face contorted. Such a horrible taste, but I loved the burning feeling as it went down. In time, that burning feeling would become all too familiar.

Many years later, Dad and I were reminiscing about the songs William taught him, and I asked something that's always puzzled me.

'If Grandad was like a republican, then why did he join the British Army and fight in the First World War?'

'To eat, son, simple as that.'

William was still a boy when, in 1916, he took the King's shilling. A young lad dressed in khaki, proudly marching off to France as an Irish Guard. I wonder if he knew what he was about to experience as he left on this foreign adventure. Did he fancy himself a hero who would win medals and honours? Or did he march blindly into the gates of hell?

I imagine blood and mud, loud screams breaking through the rattle of gunfire; mortars and grenades exploding; the smell of burning flesh, as mustard gas and death hover over a nightmare of bodies.

Did William see the faces of those he killed before they fell in the dirt?

I wonder if he cried or just held it in? I hope he had a way of escaping the horrors – perhaps a dream of galloping through the fields of Mayo to hold his sweetheart Theresa in his arms. Did he have a tattered photo of her and a picture of the sacred heart of Jesus in his pocket? Maybe there was a letter to remind him of what normal once was – maybe a last cigarette before he went over the top yet again. Did he take communion in the trenches and make the sign of the cross to ask God to keep him alive?

'William,' I heard myself cry, 'would you rather have been invisible or been able to fly?'

* * *

William was wounded, blasted with shrapnel and eventually sent home. His fighting days were over, but his real battle was about to begin.

Theresa always said the man who went to war wasn't the same one who came back to her. The pain and trauma he'd experienced had given birth to a new person: a violent, hopeless alcoholic. As I write this, my mind is sliding down the strands of my DNA, and for a brief moment I'm locked in with William. It takes a shudder and a shake to break free.

The Great War produced generations of alcoholics, both men and women. My dad told me that, when he was a boy, the pub at the end of the street would open at five o'clock in the morning, so people could have a drink and work without withdrawing.

Another of Dad's stories was about Mrs O'Malley. On Friday nights, he and his big brothers would watch through an upstairs sash window as she toddled up the hill to the pub. She'd have a tin jug concealed under her shawl that the barman would fill with stout. By the time Mrs O'Malley was on her third trip, she'd be slipping and sliding in her clogs, banging off the walls, blind drunk. The boys laughed their heads off at this wonderful live entertainment – through a window rather than a TV screen!

Then there was the kindly Mrs Doyle, who would go from house to house, visiting the sick. However, if she thought someone was near the end, she'd take a penny policy out so she could cash it in when they died. You didn't want her turning up like the grim reaper, weighing the odds when you were rough (then coming to the funeral to have a good drink!).

Another character was the knocker-upper, whose long stick would bang on bedroom windows in the early hours to wake up Grandad and his fellow workers for their shifts in the mills, pits and factories of our dark northern town. Dad would describe smoke pouring from hundreds of chimneys, and the thunderous clatter of clogs on the cobbled streets. He'd tell of gaslights being manually lit every night and extinguished in the morning, and the milkman doing his daily rounds by horse and cart. And how on Sundays everyone would go to Mass before all the men trooped off to the pub – a guaranteed scrap every week, without fail.

Dad was the youngest of four boys and would have been one of eight, had nature not reclaimed her children. I wonder how Theresa survived such tragedy, but it seems her faith never wavered: she was a woman of prayer and attended church every day.

Not that bereavement was her only challenge. Grandad's clogs, which were black with metal tips on the end, left their mark on her and the boys. Perhaps that contributed to my uncle Bill becoming a professional boxer. As his mum didn't like him fighting, he took the somewhat ironic name of Snowball Williams. One day, my dad told me, Bill calmly pushed Grandad against the wall and said, 'That's the last time you'll ever lay a hand on my mam again.' It was. The violence stopped, but the drinking didn't. Grandma had to wait outside the factory gates with the other wives on payday, otherwise a week's wages would be poured into broken vessels and spilled out in anger and resentment.

Grandad's wounds caused him constant pain. He would wake up screaming, gasping for air, his nightmare real, every day.

In 1950, with a bottle of whisky by his side, William Fleming said his last prayer. He knelt down in front of the oven at work, turned on the gas and placed his head inside. His body was discovered by a local bobby doing his rounds, who reported, 'He was in a kneeling position, holding his rosary as though praying.' I imagine the glass beads hung in mid-air, like teardrops suspended in time. Somehow, I know how he felt in his final moments. I've lived to die myself.

I think William chose to be invisible because he couldn't fly any more.

Grandad and Grandma were devout Catholics and suicide is seen as a mortal sin. Grandma believed Grandad was in hell. She said he 'died like a dog' and she wouldn't allow his name ever to be mentioned in the house. She lived in shame, but prayed for mercy for him for the rest of her life.

I never knew him, but I love him, I know him; he's me and I'm him.

* * *

Recently, the BBC asked me to do a podcast about my upbringing, and one of my sisters and I shared our memories of growing up. At the end, the host surprised us with something we never knew: Grandad was the first person in the UK to get done for drink driving. He ran over someone when he was drunk on his motorbike.

In court, the policeman said: 'Fleming smelled strongly of drink and was slurring his words.'

Grandad put up a robust, if unusual, defence: 'It was the smell of steak and kidney pudding I'd had for lunch, not alcohol, your honour.'

Sadly, you don't get drunk on steak and kidney puddings.

William lost the case and got a fine.

Life and death, alcohol and steak and kidney puddings, love and loss … Grandad's story is part of me.

His clogs continue to echo on the cobbles of Burnley.

9
WHERE NORMAL LIVES

I WANT TO FEEL HUMAN AGAIN. I'm lost. I don't think I can do this. It's just too hard.

Voices hammering on the inside of my head, fighting to escape the prison I've built for myself. I know every face. I know all their stories, their cries, even in my quietest moments. Waking up in the darkness, unable to breathe, drowning in a sea of bodies as waves of fear crash over me. I feel hands grabbing my feet and legs, pulling me under, holding me down. Voices of sobbing children, screams of grieving mothers, piercing every inch of my being.

The battle to break free. To run far away and find a place where normal lives and death only comes after a long, happy life. A place of smiles, where children eat every day, and mums sleep soundly, unconstrained by the dark hand of homelessness that pins many to the wall.

I think I lived in this magical land once, many years ago. I remember feeling safe, holding on to Mum and Dad and laughing as they swung me back and forth. Thoughts of ice cream and sandcastles. The door of the Formica kitchenette open, revealing packets and potions and rolling pins. Mum's homemade jam slice and the smell of buns slowly cooking in the oven. Licking the cake mixture from the large beige bowl – how heavy it was – and Mum's smiling eyes as my head emerged with the evidence all over my face.

Sometimes I wonder, was it real? Or am I just super-imposing a dream world on top of this black and white nightmare?

My mental health has always been fragile at times. I've often felt like jumping and sometimes I've craved it. Medicines seem to steady me, but the downside is they make me feel as if I'm seeing the world without knowing what I'm looking at, and that's almost worse.

Slumped exhausted in an empty church, I pull the dog collar from my neck and hold it like a knife. I run it across the inside of my arm, imagining the satisfying release of warm blood running down my pale skin and dripping to the floor.

But though those thoughts are there, they aren't real any more. I smile to myself as I remember my last stay in a mental health unit – the nurses, the support, my friends …

Time to get back to reality.

Oh, but it's been such a long day! Another suicide, another grieving family. So much sorrow. Men and women just queuing up to die.

I'm going to do something about it, even if it kills me, even if I die trying, God help me!

Do I really want to help all the mentally ill people I know, I wonder, or do I really need help myself? If I need to be needed and so do they, maybe we can survive together. This begins to seem like an excellent compromise.

* * *

As I started to investigate how churches stop suicides, I found a lot of debate on the subject but no real action. I pondered, I prayed. I thought of my time in mental health units, lost in that darkness I couldn't speak of to anyone. There were drugs to hide my fear and to dull the voices that seemed to deceive me. What was I really in need of then?

My life had been like a warm, running bath. The water was relaxing and the tub large and luxurious, but no one had thought to put the plug in. Every form of help just washed away down the drain.

What if there was more co-operation? What about a drug and alcohol unit working hand in hand with a mental health unit and a homeless unit, the professionals all under one roof, available to everyone, with no appointments necessary?

A twenty-first-century monastery, I thought. Boosh, that's it!

The idea felt so right.

Twenty-four hours later, it became obvious that the NHS, the drug and alcohol services and the homeless services weren't getting on board for the party. By that time, though, I was burning inside: nothing was going to stop me now.

'Ed, I need the BBC to come and do a piece on mental health. Can you help?'

The legend that is Ed Thomas and the truly amazing cameraman Phil Edwards turned up ready for action. They followed me for a couple of weeks and produced an award-winning documentary, revealing the desperate need for mental health care to be easily accessible to all. Within hours of the programme airing, the phone lines were lighting up non-stop and the twenty-first-century monastery was born.

It's called Church on the Street.

There had been many meetings and diverse conversations, but it was pretty much handshakes and nods that seemed to do the trick. The day came when I realised, amid the bustle of professionals and heartbroken people flocking for help, that the dream was alive – and so was I. I looked around the room and saw a real church.

As I thanked God, my attention was drawn to a lady gliding across the floor. She flicked back her hair, put her bag down and seated herself with the mental health professionals. I lifted my glasses to rub my eyes and refocus. Her ruby red lips gave her away … my old nurse on the ward all those years ago! She didn't really remember me. I'd been one of thousands, after all, but it was her. She was a type of supervisor now. The years had been kind and she spoke with confidence.

What a strange twist of fate, I thought.

And then the male practitioner beside her said, 'Do you remember me, Mick? I nursed you on the wards.'

* * *

Twelve months later, those wonderful professionals won a special NHS award for their work with us. As we all sat round a table at the ceremony, relaxing and celebrating, I felt somehow complete. I lifted my orange juice in a toast to my Lord and Saviour, Jesus Christ.

The work at Church on the Street had previously caught the attention of the Prince and Princess of Wales. They came to visit us, and have continued to support and help us in what we do. It was thrilling to receive an email inviting myself and Sarah to Westminster Abbey for the Princess of Wales's Christmas concert.

The day came and there we were, me and Sarah, in London on a cold December afternoon, having a stroll along the South Bank before the big event. All at once, I could smell a protest, and the next thing you know, we'd joined in! 'Save our NHS,' we chanted – something that's so important to us both. The old fire was burning as we all marched and protested in unison, and I didn't want to leave. But Sarah grabbed my hand and pulled me from the crowd.

'We have to get to the abbey, Mick, or we won't get in.'

'OK, love, let's go.'

The queue outside snaked for what looked like miles. I felt cold, not like when I was on the march, but when we finally entered the door to the abbey, tickets in hand … What a ceiling! Feelings of awe deepened with every piece of art my eyes feasted on. How could people construct a place of such beauty? I felt so small in that glorious space, like a fly buzzing in a cake shop.

Me and Sarah moved slowly along the north aisle, and when we were about halfway down, we were approached by a perfectly turned-out man in a blue suit. I noticed a medal pinned to his jacket. The shine on his black shoes told me he must have been a soldier once. He was standing straight, his shoulders back, his white hair cropped to perfection.

'But your tickets are pink,' he said in a surprised tone, as his eyes looked me up and down. He seemed troubled by my pink tickets and asked who I was. Then he led us to another gentleman with the same impeccable appearance. My clothes never look like that! My shoes don't shine that way even when they're brand new. I wondered why. Maybe it's in how you wear them.

But those shoes were carrying me and Sarah ever nearer the front. I happened to look at her just as she glanced at me. To our right we could see two regal chairs, and twenty or so that were less regal but different to the others laid out in the abbey. Sarah leaned into my ear.

'Is that the King and Queen's chair, Mick?'

'I think so, love. Surely we're not going to be …'

But the pink tickets did the trick. One minute we were chanting 'Save the NHS', the next we were being seated right smack bang in the middle of the seats reserved for the royal family in Westminster Abbey!

It's a strange life, mine. And then it got even stranger. A tap on the shoulder, and I turned to a very polite lady with a beautifully modulated voice.

'Pastor Mick, the Princess would like to speak with you.'

'No problem, love, that'll do for me.'

Not quite the same etiquette back but a warm smile and a nod nonetheless.

And there she was – a real princess. She shook my hand and held it as we spoke about mental health. She even thanked me for being there. When I sat back down, the seats around ours had begun to fill. Nods and smiles towards us. I couldn't help smiling back, wondering if the onlookers assumed we were some long-lost royal relatives …

I can't remember much about the concert but when it finished, the problems began. You see, the royal party leave first and process down the nave, past the entire congregation, and we were in the royal party, just behind the King and Queen. Sarah was completely overtaken by the moment and began nodding, waving and smiling at people as we walked by. I had trouble holding it together, myself! Then at the door, there was a queue as each couple's motor car drew up. Newspaper photographers and TV cameras filled the night sky with flickers and lights as they clicked and filmed away.

When the Range Rovers and Rolls Royces had left, our turn came. We proudly walked by the paparazzi, who continued snapping as Sarah paused and smiled. I had to drag her away to the bus stop.

That night I had a dream. I was sitting on top of thousands of different shoes, trying them on and finding none would fit. When I woke up in the morning, though, I realised I didn't need to look for any more shoes.

I already have the right pair.

10
BABY STEPS

I DON'T THINK FAIRNESS and equality really exist in life. I've seen so much injustice and tried to work out if pain ever ends. Jesus seems to show us that by going through, not around, troubles and holding fast to truth, we can find freedom. If Jesus died for my sins, then first I must know what they are.

Yet, it's painful when they are revealed. I used to feel so bad and full of shame and guilt and almost tried to hide away. Then something changed. I realised that if Jesus died for my sins, then I should be glad when my sins are exposed, because I am being set free.

Game changer.

I became grateful for the pain.

'Thank you, Jesus, for showing me who I am!'

And so fairness stopped being a measure. I realised that, in the end, all that matters is love – God's love reflecting through us, in troubles, in joy – it's always love. My old mum, God bless her soul, was right all along.

Well, obviously. She had to put up with me all her life!

* * *

A few years ago, a lad I'd met on the psychiatric ward came to one of our recovery groups with a dark-haired girl called Emily. Right away I could see something different about her.

There was a spark in those deep brown eyes, a warmth in the ready smile that made it so easy and comfortable to talk to her. Yet, as I got to know Emily over the next few months, I began to sense an inner sadness and desperation. I wondered what her story was. So one day I asked her.

'How long have you got, Mick?'

'As long as it takes, Emily.'

* * *

Emily grew up in Haslingden, a northern town where old weavers' cottages nestle near a reservoir. Her playground was the hills and moors around her home and she loved roaming there.

'I was quite feral!' she told me. 'I would think nothing of bringing my mum a sheep's scull home as a present!'

She loved the seaside too and would often go and stay with her grandma and grandad, who had a bed and breakfast in Blackpool. Her days were spent running on the sands, chasing the seagulls, splashing in the waves, collecting shells on the shoreline ... Then, full of fresh sea air, she would fall asleep in an instant, dreaming of tomorrow.

When Emily was about ten, her grandparents decided to turn some of their property into flats. They rented one to a family friend and her nineteen-year-old son.

Catastrophe.

The teenager began to expose himself to Emily when they were alone on the beach, and over the next couple of years, things only got worse. He'd take what Emily thought were pink balloons out of his bedroom drawer and make her go with him to the bathroom. Barricaded in against her will, her innocence was brutally stolen.

1 Mick's great-uncle and grandad   2 Mum and toddler Mick

3 Mick and sister Sarah   4 Mick and dad

5 Mick and mum   6 Mick with eldest boys

7 Mick as Elvis   8 Mick at his graduation

9 Mick and dad   10 Ozzy, the wonder dog

11 The Prince and Princess of Wales visiting COTS

12 Jeremy Vine and Mick   13 Mick with Sir Bryn Terfel

14 Mick on BBC Radio 4 *Saturday Live*

5

6

15 Mick at his consecration   16 Mick at Lambeth Palace Library

17 Mick at Palace Garden Party   18 Sarah at Palace Garden Party

19 'Together at Christmas' Carol Service

20 Mick in Paris   21 Mick on French book tour

22 Mick's youngest son, Jack   23 Clara with Mick

24 Ed Thomas with Mick   25 Emily at COTS

26 Chris's painting   27 Mick with Chris Difford and Kev Whittaker

When a young girl is being forced to behave like a woman, she loses all connection with her friends and with people her own age, and feels utterly isolated. Emily did try to speak to her grandma. But having grown up at a time when abuse was generally brushed under the carpet, her grandma's first response was to protect the family.

'Don't tell your grandad. It will kill him.'

Emily never did. Long before her grandad died fifteen years later, she had learned to keep her mouth shut and her emotions on ice. She was still in her teens when she began to turn to the confidence builder, the liar, that pretended to be her best friend: alcohol. Emily would drink to oblivion and get into scraps and fights. Bottles of cider and fumbles on the park bench led her into womanhood.

She found it a place without love.

Partners came and went and were often violent. Covering bruises and cuts became a normal part of putting on her make-up. It was difficult not to feel that the vile words spoken over her defined who she was; to believe the lie about herself.

Evil does that. It destroys you, then blames you for unravelling, even getting you to say thank you. When evil calls itself love, you have been truly deceived and beaten.

* * *

Emily found what seemed the perfect job: she became an escort. She would wake up in cheap hotels wrapped naked in stained sheets – a world of pine mirrors, bedside lamps and crappy pictures on the walls, one room just melting into another. The morning shower was warm, but couldn't wash away the stench of self-loathing … the smell of bacon and eggs tormented her that normality was just a slice of toast away. Then the familiar taxi journey home, with peering eyes in the driver's mirror, judging but never speaking.

Human beings are fickle creatures. It seems so easy to give love, but to really receive it is far more difficult. Emily was screaming, 'Love me!' but no longer felt capable of being loved herself. There needed to be some kind of rebirth, and that came with children.

'Holly-Louise looked like a little angel. When I held her in my arms, and our eyes met, I could feel love pouring in. I began to sense there was some hope of life beginning again.'

Every little step Holly took, Emily took with her – it was as if they were walking baby steps together. When babies are learning, sometimes they fall, get back up and toddle on. It was like that for Emily too, but now her days were full of colour and meaning.

However, Holly-Lousie had been born with a progressive illness, and the two-year-old suddenly became desperately ill. Emily held her as she passed away in the most tragic of circumstances. She was left with pictures in her mind that mothers are just not meant to carry.

Slipping into an alcoholic stupor, she temporarily lost her sanity and found herself on her knees in the graveyard, clawing away the dirt.

'I just wanted to hold and cuddle my beautiful baby one last time, Mick.'

* * *

Today, Emily can hardly recognise the person she once was. Even though she still has mental struggles and has to take medication for bipolar, she thinks of herself as a strong woman. She feels lucky that she's come through so much; that her addiction has not defined her; that she can advocate for others who are suffering in the way she did.

Emily still goes back to the seaside. That childlike enchantment with the natural world will never leave her.

Like me, she's learned the hard way that love is the only thing you can keep by giving it away.

But I've never before met a woman who buys the gulls their own chips!

That's Emily for you.

11
HEART TO HEART

'DON'T MOVE. JUST LIE DOWN. You've had a massive heart attack. Just rest.'

The doctor's words didn't seem to be having much effect on me. I looked up at the lights in the ceiling and noticed that one kept flickering. Somehow it took me back to when my mum passed away and that brought very uncomfortable emotions. I was in the same hospital, but this was a different time. Right now, I was stuck here – in my purple shirt and clerical collar – with nurses and doctors pronouncing words that felt pointless.

'Can I go home and get my dog Ozzy sorted out?'

'Mr Fleming, this is serious. You could die.'

I looked at the doctor's stony face, his brushed-back black hair. His dark eyes seemed to flicker in time with the faulty light. I checked his lips but there was no movement, no sign of a smile. He'd become like the environment, clinical and businesslike.

My mind slowly began to catch up with the severity of the situation as the nurse wrapped an alien creature round my arm and pumped it full of air. Then, as she put a peg on the end of my finger, a memory opened up right in front of me: Mum singing as she pegged the washing out on the line, socks dancing, towels drying in the breeze. And me as a child, sat on the step, looking at the shapes in the clouds in the sky.

When I blinked, I was back in the ward. I noticed the nurse had long curly red hair and green eyes, but her beauty was in her smile. Soft pink lips curving to reveal white teeth … My heart felt Irish as I remembered all the rebel songs my dad and uncles used to sing after a skinful of ale. Peace began to consume me. Warmth enfolded. And then came joy.

'Give us a dance, nurse.'

A moment of connection before she turned to leave the room with a little flick of her cream shoes.

Left alone, I was overtaken by a feeling of ecstasy and a song burst out of me, like I had no control over it: 'Bless the Lord, oh my soul, oh, oh, oh my soul. I worship your holy name …'

On repeat, over and over again, getting louder and louder. I felt a strange kind of freedom, far beyond human knowing. If this was a taste of death, I was ready. I was almost craving it …

A swish of air from the door and the doctor stood next to me. He looked puzzled. He couldn't understand what was happening. His eyes questioned my mental health, and I've no doubt his ears had reservations about my out-of-tune symphony.

'Could I ask, Mr Fleming, why you seem to be so happy?' He gazed directly into my eyes, as if searching for answers. 'It's a very serious matter. You have several blood clots in your main arteries. Any one of them could end your life. Why are you singing and smiling?'

'Are you a man of faith, doctor?' I asked.

'No. I believe that, like animals, when we die we just rot.' His face seemed to relax as he spoke his piece. It was as if he wanted me to know there was nothing.

But he wasn't quite sure …

'Oh, I'm so very, very sorry, doctor. I think you're so much more than that.'

'What do you mean?'

'You're so much more than an animal. You save lives. You live, you love and you have compassion.'

'Yeah, but why are you happy?'

'Because I might die. I may go home to meet my maker. You see, my life is eternal. I can't wait.'

His jaw dropped. His gaze became unsettled. His hands shook slightly and I could see lines on his forehead that hadn't been visible before. There was a moment of silence.

'If you just die and rot, it doesn't really matter what you do in life. Is there anything in your life that you're sorry for?'

He gasped for air. His gaze was downward now as he looked at his black shiny shoes.

I reached out and took his hand. 'Do you believe in Jesus?'

'I do.'

I felt his hand tighten as a tear ran down his face.

'You're so much more to God than you could ever imagine.'

He nodded and wiped his eyes. Just for a second when he turned around at the door, I could see the hint of a smile. Maybe we were both getting treatment for heart disease. Maybe both our hearts were being repaired.

* * *

After a few days of rest and some surgery, I let go of the idea of imminent death. It seemed I would be here just a little bit longer. The joy I'd experienced, however, stayed and continues to this day.

Up and about, walking through the ward, people would call me over to pray with them. It was a beautiful time and I felt richly blessed. So many visitors, so many well-wishers and messages. The people who really loved me were troubled and worried, but I wasn't. I thought I'd better behave though, because I didn't want Sarah telling me off. I'd take it easy ... ish.

My final night in hospital gave me the chance to reflect on my life, and my mind and heart were filled with people I'd known, with stories, with loves and hopes and fears. In that moment I really missed my own mother ... her protection, her love, her understanding. She knew how to make it better. Homemade pies, proper chips. All of us sat around the dinner table. My sisters shouting, 'Mum, he's kicking us under the table.'

I remember eating as quickly as possible so I could lay claim to the biggest piece of homemade jam pastie. My dad's calloused hand would be holding a pint pot of tea, as he warmed himself up from a cold, wild day trying to make a living from cleaning windows. My beautiful mum, holding everything together, there at the cooker.

I can see my sister Anne dancing in the living room, singing 'Crazy Horses' by the Osmonds, cheekily changing the word 'horses' to 'arses' and my mum shouting, 'I'll wash your mouth out with soap.'

A family, a belonging. All gone now. Yet death always leaves something behind.

I guess it's what you do with what's left.

* * *

'How are you feeling, Mr Fleming?' The nurse brought my thoughts back to the present.

'Amazing, nurse. Thanks.'

'We heard about you singing the other day. You're going home tomorrow, aren't you?'

'I hope so.'

'Can I ask you something?'

'Yes, of course.'

'Do you really think God is real?'

'Honestly. I've no doubt of that.'

As she turned, I noticed a tiny tear tattoo on her wrist. Sadness came over her as I asked about it.

'It's for my little boy. He passed away. It tears me apart.'

'Do you think you'll see him again?'

'Hope so. I'm not certain.'

'Well, I'll tell him if I get there first.'

'How can you be so sure?'

'You see this tattoo on my hand – the cross? Put your tattoo on there.'

She gently put her wrist across the back of my hand. I saw her lips quiver and she looked away, but her wrist rested where it was.

'Everything you've ever done in your life – would you trade it for love?'

'Yes, I would,' she said.

The green eyes welled up as I asked her if she would give her little boy to Jesus to look after. She turned her hand over and held mine. And as she looked at the cross on my hand, she breathed out.

'Yes, yes, I will. I feel love … what's happening to me?'

We were both in tears now.

Funny that. My dodgy heart being treated by people whose hearts are being healed by Jesus.

Life is so strange. How can someone's pain play a part in transforming other people's lives? Somehow, I just think it's not the pain. It's the *sharing* of the pain that brings healing. And understanding who and what Jesus is.

As we come together, unable to fix ourselves, unsure about who and what we really are, all we have is the story of the cross. The Jesus story that transforms and changes lives, as we go through the pain and come out to a resurrected life.

You know, within a week of leaving hospital, I was flying in a plane.

Not advisable. But you only live twice.

That's my motto anyway.

12
THE TIME TRAVELLER

'WE'RE GOING TO NEED YOU to come to London to promote the book, Mick.'

'OK,' I said.

Blown Away, my autobiography, opened up new worlds for me. For the first time in my life, I felt grown up as I hopped on planes, trains and buses to places I'd never visited before – in this country, in Europe and even as far away as Africa.

Before my trip to London in 2022, I could scarcely remember being on a train – just a vague recollection of Mum and Dad telling me off for bouncing up and down on the seat of a steam one on holiday. Strange how little life experience I've had in the so-called 'normal world'.

Walking into Preston station, I was immediately overwhelmed by the size of the place. The light shining through the glass roof was dazzling, but I could see the platform was crowded. A group of middle-aged men in expensive suits chatted as they leant on long-handled suitcases on wheels. Glancing down at my zip-up sports bag – packed with three pairs of underpants and socks, two shirts and a New King James Bible – I wondered if I was doing this travelling thing wrong.

As the train pulled in with a thunderous sort of whooshing sound, my eyes travelled the length of it – an entire alphabet of letters in red squares on the side of carriages that seemed to stretch for miles. I pulled my ticket from my shirt pocket and surveyed the numbers and letters for at least the fiftieth time.

H27.

The train juddered to a halt and a strange change seemed to come over the waiting crowd. Old men took on the sprightly aspect of prize fighters; a woman in high heels stood tall, poised and ready – she wasn't going to hold back! I stood almost frozen as people jostled for position. Then the magic doors opened and funnelled everyone inside.

Throwing my grey bag over my shoulder, I felt the thud of the Bible as it hit me in the middle of my spine. I dashed to locate the elusive H27, but when I finally found it, someone was already sitting there.

Is that allowed? I thought. *What do I do? What's the protocol?*

My head said, *Oi, fat lad, shift it.* But my mouth did a better job. 'Excuse me, I think this is my seat.'

Clutching the ticket with the special numbers on, I waved it in front of his eyes. No verbal response except a deep sigh, before he grabbed his cheese and onion crisps and laptop case. The journey to London had begun.

* * *

As the train cut through the countryside, I noticed myself trying to count the sheep in the fields. But we were going much too quickly, so I put my head against the window and quietly prayed. A lady with a brown birthmark on her cheek came and sat next to me. She smelled expensive, and I noticed that the little bag over her shoulder matched the suitcase she lifted on to the rack above our heads.

What do you do on a train when someone sits so close to you – especially a lady? Do you speak? Make polite conversation about nothingness? Or just pretend they're not there? I was at a loss, but then a terrible feeling began to consume me. My stomach was making strange sounds as the wind inside fought to break free. I squirmed in my chair and eventually breathed easy again as my bodily functions (temporarily) calmed down.

As we pulled into Euston station, everyone grabbed their cases and poured out on to the platform. I picked up my bag and shuffled through the door. No sooner had my feet hit the concrete than everything that had been held in exploded! Thank goodness, the sound was masked by the thunder of those rolling wheels, along with an ocean of different voices from all across the globe.

I looked across the concourse, lost and a bit fearful. But there she was, waiting for me: Alison, the book lady, better known to others as the publisher. She took my arm and led me through the chaos, out into the street. Wow! The sun glittered off tall glass buildings (we don't have those in Burnley), and in the hustle and bustle for a taxi, a kindly driver beckoned us to the front of the queue. He seemed to know who I was, and that gave me pause for thought. A complete stranger in a strange city, and yet not a stranger at all ...

The hotel was near Westminster, and as we strolled around before dinner, I saw Big Ben in real life for the first time. It looked brand new (turned out, it had just had an £80 million makeover), and the whole of the Palace of Westminster was stunning. Just for a second, I began to count the glass windows and wondered if any politicians had ever been chucked in the river! Just one of those random strange thoughts that come unprompted ...

The next day, we were off to the BBC to do the Jeremy Vine show on Radio 2. Though I don't have a TV or radio myself, I'd definitely heard of Jeremy, and what a lovely guy he was. He introduced me by playing Johnny Cash singing 'The Man in Black' – one of my favourite songs for many reasons – and our interview went on for about half an hour. When we came out of the studio, he kindly filmed a little video for my sister Marie, who's one of his biggest fans.

The following morning, I shared the airwaves with Mel C from the Spice Girls, jewellery designer Theo Fennell and opera singer Rebecca Bottone – all of them 'sound' – as Revd Richard Coles and Nikki Bedi hosted us on *Saturday Live*. Afterwards we went to the café beside Broadcasting House for a restorative caffeine shot, and found Richard and Nikki had had the same idea!

Blown Away became a bestselling book, and within a year it had been translated into French. I was invited to Paris for the launch of *Rédemption: Du deal à la vraie Vie* (*Redemption: From the deal to real life*).

The publisher had arranged for me to speak and sign books at a Catholic outdoor festival in a place called Paray-le-Monial, where Jesus is said to have revealed his sacred heart to a French nun, many years ago. Little did the organisers and I anticipate what an incredible experience the next few days would be. When we met and they asked me to run through what I would be saying, I told them I didn't know: I would just trust God to give me the right words when the time came. A professional interpreter, a lovely lady with a soft voice that was very calm and soothing, asked if I would be able to speak slowly: a Burnley accent doesn't travel too well in French.

In the course of the day, I began to realise that the organisers thought I was a Catholic bishop. I decided to just ride it out and see what God did in this beautiful place. When the time came for me to stand up in front of thousands of people (none of them with English as a first language), I gazed up at the early evening sky and then down at the sea of bodies on the grass – some sitting on plastic chairs, others leaning against the trees – and prayed, 'Lord, please speak for me.'

Time stood still. For a moment, the silence was complete. Even the breeze stopped blowing. Then I caught the eye of the translator and she nodded. I took a deep breath.

'Jesus loves prostitutes.'

The nice lady hesitated for a moment. Then a gasp arose from the crowd and hit the stage. A symphony of tears began to roll around the far corner of the gathering, and as the sound gathered momentum, it was as if God had spoken directly into the hearts of many people.

'That's right. Jesus loves prostitutes. He loves drug addicts, and he loves you.'

The words were coming out of my mouth, but I was completely unaware that there were thousands of women in the audience who had been sex trafficked. The organisers had encouraged them to come to the festival, but no one had ever told them that Jesus loved them. As the reality of the gospel took hold, the crowd surged forward and priests began to appear. People gathered in line for prayer and a touch of hope, and these pastors prayed individually with many broken souls.

I placed my hand on one lady's head and said simply, 'Be loved.' She fell to her knees, and a lifetime of tears watered the scorched grass. Simultaneously, singing broke out and we worshipped into the night. The language didn't seem to matter; the religiosity didn't exist; we just knew the love of God calling us into his embrace.

The morning after, as I signed many books, I understood the French title in a whole new way. In English, I am blown away. In French, I am redeemed. And in German, with that edition (*Schonungslose Gnade*) now published too, I have received ruthless grace.

I think Jesus speaks all languages to all people; we only need to learn to listen.

13
A CHRISTMAS MIRACLE

THE COLD WINDS WRAP AROUND his body, like a spiteful lover. The dark echo of his breath slowly disappearing into a distant silence. The familiar smell of an old friend who would never desert him lay heavy on his breath. Home on the street, but no door and never a key. Once a father, never a son. Flashes of a man that never was. A victim from the age of eleven. A child that forgot how to cry. Nightmares that unpacked but would never leave. To sleep, to smile, to feel the touch of humanity, were all things for others. Finding a god in a needle and love in a pipe.

How much longer?

He asks for nothing and receives it in abundance.

Flashing lights. A strange unfamiliar warmth. Distant voices. A brilliant blinding blackness. No one to cry. No one to leave flowers. A nameless face, neither forgotten nor remembered.

Then the wind blew again, and they all turned away.

Readers of *Blown Away* may recall that this is what I miraculously managed to put down on paper when asked, many years ago now, these two questions: *What does it feel like to live the kind of life you live? And what do you think the future holds?*

The experience of being desperately lonely, of having no hope for the future, of feeling you're simply waiting to die … this is a reality for thousands of people who just can't break free. I'll always be grateful that something changed in my life, even though it happened very slowly.

First, I had to slip into insanity in order to encounter anything that resembled compassion. There isn't much love in the world for drug addicts and alcoholics, you see. We are the lepers; we are the thief on the cross. But though we crave death, God offers life. And when Jesus becomes real to us, we can learn how to focus on God even in our trials.

'Where are you looking for me, Mick?' I often hear Jesus call. 'I'm here!'

During the years when I was lost, the thing I most feared was people. It's so difficult to make sense of who we are when we're in pain and trauma, but it seemed to me that I had to hurt others before they could hurt me. The result was that I created my own prison and blamed the world for locking the cell door. Even now, I prefer my own company. When it's just me and Ozzy the wonder dog I find myself thinking I don't really like people. Yet, when I intervene and refuse to dwell in the darkness of inner isolation, I feel fulfilled and whole. Freedom and joy are to be found in living in Christ or, as the apostle Paul says, *en Christo*.

* * *

For well over a year now, I've been sharing daily messages and thoughts with Chris. He and I met through Church on the Street in Preston, and though we see each other briefly face to face each week, it's our correspondence that has bonded us together in a wonderfully strong way. I wonder why it has taken me years to find another human being who just seems to get me! I get him too. I like Chris. I really do.

His full story is too much for a human being to hear, let alone experience. I think I maybe love him because my desperate poem is also his. And yet the truth is that both of us have discovered a new verse – one which allows for all we're still carrying, which allows us to fall from time to time, but which ultimately reveals a truth we simply didn't know before: the cross brings life not death.

* * *

Chris first used drugs when he should have been in bed waiting for Santa. And it was at Christmas time thirteen years ago that everything changed. I'll never forget the day he told me his extraordinary story.

We were sitting in the cabin he'd built on what had been an overgrown, rubble-filled area in the middle of Preston. For six years, he's laboured to create a little oasis of peace. I wondered where his drive had come from; why he'd felt compelled to devote so much time to this project. After all, he had a house elsewhere to live in.

'Some days I didn't want to come and do anything, but I did. That's the key, Bishop: keep going.'

Chris rolled a cigarette. It looked a bit like a miniature Christmas tree, with branches hanging out the end. As he lit it and took a drag, he told me he 'f***ing loved Jesus'.

You know what? I felt so connected. I felt I could just be me. The kettle boiled, steam filling the room, before it clicked itself off. Then a proper brew – hot, sweet and tanned.

'I'll show you round the rec, Bishop,' he said, 'OK?'

We grabbed our builder's mugs of tea and went outside for a moment. I could see raised beds of plants – gold, red, pink and purple – held in blue timber frames. There was a large, grassed area, bordered with a flagged path, and beautiful bushes overlooked the entire space.

Back in the cabin, Chris suddenly said, 'What's that? Can you feel it?'

With each breath, we were conscious of becoming calmer and more at peace. We hadn't done anything at all … it was a Holy Spirit moment, such as I've experienced so many times before. (Funnily enough, these only ever seem to happen when the conversation is about God – never when I'm talking about football or boxing!)

'So, how did you find God, Chris?'

His piercing blue eyes sparked as I asked the question. His voice sped up with excitement, as it always does when he talks about Jesus.

* * *

Thirteen years ago Chris was at an all-time low. His relationship was over, and the drugs simply weren't working any more.

'If I put enough into me, it always seemed I could squash the pain, no matter what. But this time, the pain was just too big.'

Chris became homeless, and that prompted an even deeper spiral.

'I was taking anything. Stuff like the byproduct of amphetamine and ecstasy that no one else wanted.'

As you know, I've been around the block, but I was shocked. The byproduct of those drugs is poison, pure poison. Chris was taking his life into his own hands, and he really didn't care. Inevitably, he went into coronary arrest. When his heart had calmed down sufficiently, he carried on using, and before long he had a huge heart attack.

'It was like being engulfed in complete darkness. I could feel evil all around, above me, below me, like every wicked person or thing that had ever been was choosing to be there, and I was petrified. I just can't describe it – the images, the voices, the vile smell ... I think I met the devil in that moment.'

Chris had previously experienced psychosis. He'd had trips induced by drugs, but this was different: this felt real.

'Then I heard a voice, a demonic voice, telling me, "You have a choice: you can live or die. But if you choose life, then you belong to me. And I will be calling on you."

'It felt like I was in hell. Time didn't exist – a minute, a year – it was irrelevant. There were simply no constraints at all. And something deep down inside me said, "Choose death."'

The next thing he remembers is quite surreal. He was looking down at himself from above. 'My body was lying beside a railway track. Yet despite the distance, I was still me, with all my feelings and emotions.'

I leant forward and grabbed my tea – a comfortingly mundane action as the shivers played up and down my spine.

'My mouth was covered in grit from the embankment. I felt the roughness as I wiped it away from my mouth. And suddenly I was back in my body.'

Someone had called the police, and it was mayhem.

'Turns out I'd tried to run head on into a train. I begged the police to put cuffs on me because the demonic voice kept saying, "You're mine," and the terror was overwhelming.'

The moment the cuffs were on, Chris felt instant relief and a sense of calm.

'To this day, I've never picked up another drink or drug because I truly believe there's far more to this world than just the material.'

The truth is that though Chris had had no intention or desire to stop using, the divine had intervened. Then, out of nowhere, two days later, the rattle (withdrawal) kicked in. He was seriously ill for almost a month and his mental health took a dip. The doctors in A&E called him into a side room and shut the door. As Chris looked around, he realised there was no handle on the inside and the chair was fixed to the floor. *Here we go again*, he thought.

I asked him if he'd spent much time in psychiatric units down the years, and he told me there are at least five years of his life that he can't remember at all. Yet he feels now that, even in those dark times, God was looking out for him.

'You know, if I hadn't been in mental health units and prisons, there would have been some pretty horrific things happening to other people.'

Chris now relies totally on God for his protection. His violent days are behind him. Yet I still wanted to know how he really came to faith.

'It was close to Christmas,' he said, 'and there was a guy I was looking for.' Though Chris was now clean, he was still mentally ill and living his old ways.

'I really wanted to damage him. I'd a blade wrapped in a piece of newspaper, hidden in my boot. To be honest, I couldn't have told you what day it was; I just remember walking miles and miles.

'Next thing I knew, I was sitting outside a church. It was so cold I could see my breath, and I thought I'd go in for a moment to get warm. The Mass had already started ... I sat at the back and my mind began to recall coming when I was a kid – me and my brother and sister, desperate to escape life at home for an hour or two. I hadn't been back to church for thirty years, but you know what, Bishop? I still knew all the words.

'I felt safe. There was something special about the beautiful pictures and statues, and especially the communion.'

Chris faced a real challenge though. Should he receive full communion – bread and alcoholic wine? He knew that one sip could kick him off and he was terrified. Nonetheless, he went up to the altar, trusting that God wanted him to receive the life blood of Christ.

'I had a clear choice: God or fear. I chose God and drank from the cup.'

Chris continues to take full communion. God is the only thing that's worked for him. Narcotics Anonymous didn't, Alcoholics Anonymous didn't, only Jesus.

'Everyone gives up on me, Mick, because I'm hard work. But he never does.'

The bishop and Chris have both decided that life is truly to be found *en Christo*.

Two people with extremely dodgy pasts, dedicated to the service of the Lord.

14
JUST TWELVE STEPS MORE

'MY NAME'S MICK and I'm an alcoholic.'

Words I've said hundreds of times in so many different meetings, all around the country. AA gave me freedom to choose a different path – not an easy one by any means, but a path that offered new choices and revelations. It fostered in me the desire to build relationships with others and above all with a God of my understanding: for me, that is Jesus Christ.

My theology is and always will be entwined with my knowledge of the Bible and how it relates to the twelve-step programme. All the steps – from powerlessness to accepting God as a way to live, to confession, repentance, making amends, being convicted daily of sin, prayer and meditation, and finally carrying a message to others (evangelism) – are grounded in Scripture. AA sees alcohol as a symptom of sin and provides a way to sobriety based on the removal of a person's character defects.

It's such a remarkable and empowering notion when you consider the sinful nature of humanity. The truth is that we need one another to know who we truly are. When one alcoholic carries a message to another, growth results. In other words, my freedom depends on telling you (a fellow alcoholic) the solution.

Individuals can choose a sponsor who will guide them through the twelve steps. Sponsor and sponsee work together on an equal basis, both sharing the most intimate parts of themselves with God and with each other. It's very much like Charles Spurgeon once said when referring to evangelism: 'One beggar telling another beggar where to find bread.'

I've experienced being sponsored and being a sponsor, and both have moved me closer to God. I've seen the impossible achieved: hopelessness replaced with hope; the fullness of God, in suffering and love, pouring into the most tragic of circumstances.

Yet, as I think about AA, I remember the faces of many men and women who couldn't or wouldn't accept a spiritual solution, and so drank themselves to death. Those who do find what they are looking for, though, give me great comfort. Let me introduce one to you now.

* * *

'Hello, my name is Kev, and I'm an alcoholic.'

I met Kev through a friend in recovery. My first impression was, 'He's as mad as a box of frogs,' and I liked him straight away. Kev's a big lad, covered in tattoos. He looked scary and his potential for violence was high. Maybe it's just part of who I am, but I feel really comfortable with people like Kev.

He talked at a million miles an hour, flitting from one subject to another, and my mind couldn't keep up. But eventually he burned out and slowed right down.

'Will you sponsor me?' he asked. 'I'm desperate. I'm clean, but if I don't do something, I'm definitely going to relapse.'

I thought for a second, and as I nodded my head, I saw a smile begin to crack his granite face. He's not really a smiler, our Kev. I didn't know at that point that the journey we would go on together, through tragedy and exhilaration, would define us and tie us together for ever in a type of brotherly bond.

Kev had no faith in anything. He was drowning in a godless world. I asked him if he had ever felt love in his life, and he told me he had, from his grandad and grandma.

'You know that love you have for them?' I asked.

'Yes.'

'That's your God.'

Kev was still for a moment. Then he rubbed his beard and smiled again.

I asked if his grandparents were dead and where he thought they were.

'Heaven.'

'Who's the boss of heaven?'

'God.'

There was a sharp intake of breath. In that moment Kev knew that God was love and that he had made a beginning.

Over the next twelve months or so, we shared many profound moments, but it was in step 3 – 'We made a decision to turn our will and our lives over to the care of God as we understand him' – that things changed for ever for Kev.

There we were, sitting at the table in his living room, tea and cake next to the Big Book, two ex-crooks offering themselves to God. As Kev said the prayer that comes at the end of the step, there was a strange noise in the room. The light from the lamp seemed to glow brighter, and I felt as if I was breathing warm loving air deep into my lungs. As the noise got louder, like a ringing in our ears, Kev looked at me.

'Can you hear it, Mick?'

'Yes, Kev.'

'Is it God?'

'I'm sure it is.'

The next thing we knew, all the darkness in our lives was being washed away and a new peace was flooding in. We were overwhelmed by love. I saw Kev as my brother, and as I felt his pain, I tasted a freedom I had touched but never quite held before. This big tough man had his head bowed, praying and thanking Jesus; he was reborn. The noise stayed all night and into the next morning. Now, whenever I pray, it returns and I know it's the same for Kev.

A few days later, he rang and asked me a question that made me smile.

We agreed to meet in a secluded car park. My fingers casually tapped the steering wheel as I waited; then a glance in the mirror told me a black car with tinted glass was drawing up alongside. A final crack of gravel as it stopped. I lowered my window and so did he. We made eye contact and he looked around nervously as I lifted a package and handed it over.

Instinctively, we burst out laughing. An ex-drug dealer and a friend with a similarly dodgy past ... I wondered what would happen if we were raided. 'I swear, officer, it's a Bible!'

Such a God. Such redemption.

* * *

As winter drew in and the cold dark nights returned, Kev's workload increased. He was employed by the council to drive wagons and he'd do overtime on the gritter trucks – extra cash to help him build a new life.

When we began the steps, I asked Kev to make a wish list of how he wanted this new life to be. He wrote:

1 To be back with Donna and the kids
2 Donna not to drink
3 A more meaningful job
4 Stay sober

These were just dreams for Kev. He felt they were unattainable. I remember saying, 'Kev, all things are possible with God.' He smiled but the words seemed to bounce off him. Little did we know what was coming next.

Kev was out gritting one cold icy evening. As he sat in his warm cab contemplating life, his thoughts were interrupted by a loud bang. He climbed on the back of the truck and peered into the hopper, the place where the grit goes in. There was a dusting of snow dotted here and there, and the moonlight allowed him to see a small red book strategically placed next to the hopper. Puzzled, Kev picked it up and headed back to the comfort of the cab. He opened his hand to look properly at the little volume, and his heart began to beat faster as the words 'New Testament and Psalms' were transplanted from the front cover into his brain …

'But it's not wet! It's completely dry,' he said out loud.

Kev called me in the early hours of the morning. He told me what had happened, but there was a twist. 'Some pages are ripped out of it,' he said.

Slowly, as my groggy eyes and ears caught up with the rest of me, I asked: 'What chapters and verses come before and after the ripped-out pages?'

When Kev told me I felt a warmth run through my body. The entire Sermon on the Mount from the Gospel of Matthew was missing.

'When you go home, Kev, read the Sermon on the Mount.'

'I will. What's happening to me, Mick?'

'I think the Holy Spirit is just quickening you, Kev.'

'It's a bit mad stuff, innit!'

'It is, Kev, yeah.'

After that, every time we met, our prayers felt stronger, more meaningful and purposeful. Although Donna and Kev lived apart, they were still very much connected. It was as if they were waiting for a miracle … life's like that; sometimes you just have to wait.

But at last, wonderful things began to happen. Donna got sober, and plans were made for them to move in together – a family at last. Kev had a grown-up son from a previous relationship and I know he regretted not being there for him. He just wanted to do better for his younger two boys.

I was in the process of finishing university and spending time on the streets, building the ministry that would become Church on the Street. When we were at the stage of creating the charity, I asked Kev to be the chairman. He seemed surprised, and humbly accepted. Pretty soon we were able to employ people and Kev was the first on my hit list. He stepped down as chairman and took up a paid role as a recovery worker.

Meanwhile Kev was progressing with the twelve steps and had reached the stage of the amends. He wanted to be reconciled to his mum, but she was very ill and had dementia.

'Mick, do you think there's any point doing the amends to Mum when she doesn't even know me?'

'Yes, Kev. You do your bit and leave it to God.'

'OK.'

Kev waited for the perfect moment, and as he gently spoke to his mum, her eyes lit up and she recognised him. She spoke coherently and accepted the amends. It was as if she was back.

Then, just as he finished talking, she was gone again. But Kev had had his moment. God granted him an everlasting memory to hold in his heart. There would be many more to come.

Donna and Kev had been growing closer, their chaotic past together almost a distant memory. They were married in a beautiful ceremony, and in that moment Kev's wish list – the impossible dream – was realised. I wish I could end here with 'and they all lived happily ever after'. But sadly, life isn't always like that.

Kev and I continued to share so much together. He supported me as I struggled when Jack's mum, Lyn, passed away. He helped me to fully understand that love hurts sometimes. He was there when my beautiful Sarah got cancer. I suppose life can be about who you sit with, and Kev sat with me and I with him.

One day, he came to see me with thrilling news. Donna had got a dream job in Australia, and they were emigrating to a brand-new life. The whole family was caught up in making plans, sorting out visas and houses, and all the practicalities of moving from one side of the world to the other.

They were about to fly off into the sunset.

When Kev and I met on Friday morning for a coffee, he was bubbling with excitement. One last man hug and 'You'll have to come out and see us', and that was it. They were due to leave early the following Tuesday. I was happy for them, though naturally sad to be losing my pal. At the same time, seeing how far he'd come with the Lord gave me real comfort.

That night I was doing a worship and healing service in church when such a strange feeling came over me. I spoke it out: 'I want to pray for someone who may have a bleed on the brain, God bless them.'

My mind returned to the service and I thought no more about it.

An hour later my phone rang.

'Mick, it's Kev. Can you come to the hospital? It's Donna. I don't know what's wrong.'

'I'm on my way, Kev.'

When I got there, Donna was unconscious and there were wires and tubes everywhere. Kev and I sat by her side, our eyes constantly on the screen, periodic beeps dulling the atmosphere.

When the doctor came in, her voice was full of compassion. 'I'm sorry, but there's no hope. The bleed on the brain is so big nothing can be done. It's the machines that are keeping her alive.'

I remember Kev just saying, 'Thank you very much for everything you've done for her.' I was stunned. My mind was bouncing all over the place. It was as if my thoughts were stammering. And then the sound of pain, shrouded in tears, poured out of Kev. I staggered towards him and just held him in my arms. It wasn't meant to end this way.

Two days later, with me standing at the bottom of Donna's bed, her dad at one side, and Kev and one of his sons at the other, Donna's life support was turned off. I can't remember what I prayed but I do recall her dad saying, 'I was there

when you came into the world, and I'll stay while you go out.'
It touched me so deeply.

Then Kev's 'I love you, Donna' as she slipped away.

* * *

Love hurts so much at times that all we can do is share our pain.

When we do, it turns into love again.

Notes

1 As reported in Jamie Grierson, 'Indefinite sentences "the greatest single stain on justice system"', *The Guardian*, 3 December 2020: https://www.theguardian.com/law/2020/dec/03/indefinite-sentences-the-greatest-single-stain-on-justice-system (accessed 5 November 2024).

2 To listen to this and see full lyrics: https://genius.com/Chris-tomlin-amazing-grace-my-chains-are-gone-lyrics (accessed 5 November 2024).

RESOURCES AND
FURTHER INFORMATION

I HOPE YOU'VE ENJOYED reading *Walk in My Shoes*. If you've been touched by anything in the book, please do contact me. My details are below, along with resources and information you may find helpful.

Pastor Mick's contact details

Email: pastormick@cots-ministries.co.uk
Twitter/X : x.com/pastorfleming
Facebook: https://www.facebook.com/mick.fleming.75/

For resources to use with this book

www.cotsministries.co.uk

The Exodus Project

Bishop Mick and Pastor Emma have developed a ground-breaking recovery programme called 'The Exodus Project'. It was born out of their 25 years' experience of addiction, mental health, recovery and Christian faith journeys, and is part of Church on the Street's Recovery Academy. For more information, please see: https://www.cots-ministries.co.uk/recovery-academy/

TV and radio coverage

BBC News

Burnley: Pastor Mick urges parties to lift child benefit cap (17.6.24)
https://www.bbc.co.uk/news/articles/c977262pn8qo

ITV News

Pastor Mick and COTS feature in this article: Ketamine addiction: Rise in young people taking Ketamine prompts health warning (8.5.24)
https://www.itv.com/news/granada/2024-05-08/ketamine-bladder-spike-in-youth-addiction-causing-life-changing-health-issues

BBC Radio Sheffield

The former gangster who found God: Pastor Mick Fleming shares his Journey of Faith story (31.10.23)
https://www.bbc.co.uk/sounds/play/p0gptqt7

Sky News

Ex-criminal enforcer turned bishop reveals how he planned to kill man who raped him as a child (28.1.23)
https://news.sky.com/story/i-was-going-to-cut-his-throat-ex-criminal-enforcer-turned-bishop-reveals-how-he-planned-to-kill-rapist-12794343

ITV This Morning

'I was blinded by an angel's light, and left my drug-dealing life behind' (20.12.22)
https://www.itv.com/thismorning/articles/i-was-blinded-by-an-angels-light-and-left-my-drug-dealing-life-behind

Press coverage

Prospect Magazine

Pastor Mick and COTS feature in this article: A good death: The decline of the pauper's funeral (14.12.24)
https://www.prospectmagazine.co.uk/ideas/a-good-death/68833/the-decline-of-the-paupers-funeral

The *Lancashire Telegraph*

Church run by former gangster collecting coats and shoes for children in poverty (6.12.24)
https://www.lancashiretelegraph.co.uk/news/24776623.church-street-helping-children-affected-poverty/

The Times

Pastor Mick and COTS feature in this article: Heroin didn't kill my son – it was a drug 100 times stronger (24.6.24)
https://www.thetimes.com/uk/crime/article/heroin-didnt-kill-my-son-it-was-a-drug-100-times-stronger-jp2xswx0v

MailOnline

Pastor Mick and COTS feature in this article: Coming to a street near *you*? Warning that Chinese-made 'Frankenstein' drug 1,000 times stronger than morphine will trigger terrifying zombieland scenes engulfing opioid-ravaged US cities (2.4.24)
https://www.dailymail.co.uk/health/article-13263157/Chinese-Frankenstein-drug-zombieland-UK.html

The Mirror

Drug dealer turned pastor gives chilling 'mass deaths' warning on UK streets (1.4.24) https://www.mirror.co.uk/news/uk-news/new-super-strength-street-drug-32488915

WalesOnline

Ex-gangster turned pastor warns of new street drug 'killing in droves' (19.3.24)
https://www.walesonline.co.uk/news/uk-news/ex-gangster-turned-pastor-warns-28848469

The Metro

'I reached for the gun – then I saw a blinding light and everything changed' (24.12.23)
https://metro.co.uk/2023/12/24/i-reached-gun-saw-a-light-everything-changed-19982279/

The *Daily Mail*

Reformed pastor Mick Fleming reveals how he planned to kill his rapist (5.10.23)
https://www.dailymail.co.uk/news/article-12597215/Reformed-pastor-Mick-Fleming-reveals-planned-kill-rapist.html

The Times

Pastor Mick and COTS feature in this article: Why we all need to talk about Gen Ket (12.9.23)
https://www.thetimes.com/article/why-we-all-need-to-talk-about-gen-ket-3cngggqdz

La Vie (a weekly French Roman Catholic magazine)

Mick Fleming : Le dealer devenu pasteur (6.9.23)
https://www.lavie.fr/christianisme/temoignage/mick-fleming-le-dealer-devenu-pasteur-90119.php

The Mirror

Pastor Mick and COTS feature in this article: Cost of dying crisis exposed: Brits are 'too poor to die' as funeral fees skyrocket (17.7.23)
https://www.mirror.co.uk/money/cost-dying-crisis-exposed-brits-30451792

MailOnline

'That kind of language is immoral': Pastor and ex-gangland criminal enforcer Mick Fleming blasts BoE chief's 'appalling' remark that people 'must accept' they're poorer after coronavirus (26.4.23)
https://www.dailymail.co.uk/news/article-12015367/Pastor-Mick-Fleming-blasts-BoE-chiefs-appalling-remark-people-accept-theyre-poorer.html

Burnley Express

Church on the Street: Burnley's Pastor Mick Fleming invited to garden party for King's Coronation (19.4.23)
https://www.burnleyexpress.net/news/people/church-on-the-street-burnleys-pastor-mick-fleming-invited-to-garden-party-for-kings-coronation-4119759

The Sun

Holy Wow: I was a gun-toting, drug dealing gangster until I was blinded by the light … now I'm a bishop and Prince William is a pal (18.12.22)
https://www.thesun.co.uk/news/20796705/drug-crime-gangster-church-bishop-prince-william/

The Washington Post

Pastor Mick and COTS feature in this article: In the city

with U.K.'s highest cost of living, leaving home to stay warm (16.12.22)

https://www.washingtonpost.com/world/2022/12/15/uk-cost-of-living-crisis-heat/

Northern Life

From Dealer to Healer (30.11.22)

https://northernlifemagazine.co.uk/from-dealer-to-healer/

Premier Christianity

Pastor Mick Fleming: 'An angel told me to forgive the man who abused me' (24.11.22)

https://www.premierchristianity.com/interviews/pastor-mick-fleming-an-angel-told-me-to-forgive-the-man-who-abused-me/14318.article

The Express

The gangster who saw the light – how Pastor Mick went from dealer to the divine (29.9.22)

https://www.express.co.uk/entertainment/books/1675774/pastor-mick-fleming-former-gangster-prince-william-kate-middleton-christianity

Awards

Church on the Street was named as the winner of an NHS Star Award by East Lancashire Health Trust for Engagement and Partnership. The award was in recognition of our work with the local NHS trust, providing an accessible drop-in Wound Care and Foot Clinic at our church in Burnley.

The Orwell Prize for Exposing Britain's Social Evils 2022: The Cost of Covid – Burnley Crisis by Ed Thomas (*BBC News*)

https://www.orwellfoundation.com/investigative/ed-thomas/

2021 Sandford St Trustees' Awards: Trustees' Content
Award – Burnley Crisis
https://sandfordawards.org.uk/2021-trustees-awards/

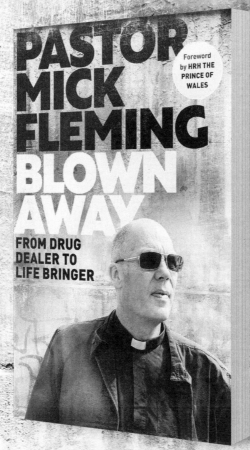